My Years With Ferrari

Also by Niki Lauda
The Art and Science of Grand Prix Driving

FRONTISPIECE: Niki Lauda studies lap times with Mauro Forghieri, Ferrari racing chief engineer. Photograph by Thomas Streimelweger.

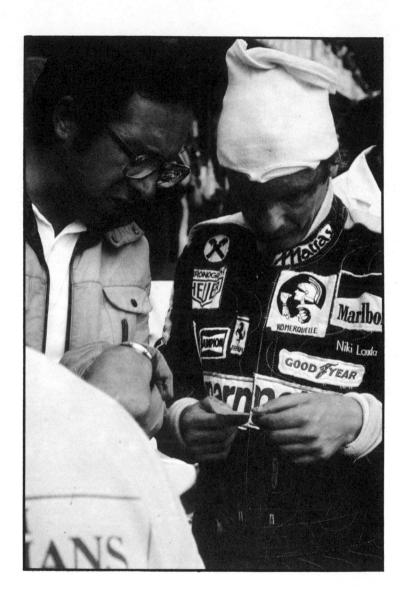

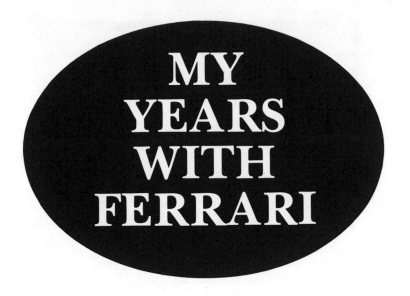

MY
YEARS
WITH
FERRARI

NIKI LAUDA

Motorbooks International
Publishers & Wholesalers Inc
Osceola, Wisconsin 54020, USA

ISBN 0-87938-059-4
Library of Congress Catalog Number 78-7559

Book text typeset by Watford Typesetters, Great Britain. Jacket and book printed and bound in the USA by the North Central Publishing Company, St. Paul.

Library of Congress Cataloging in Publication Data
Lauda, Niki, 1949–
    My years with Ferrari.

    Translation of Protokoll.
    British ed. published under title: For the record.
    1. Lauda, Niki, 1949–   2. Automobile racing drivers—Biography. 3. Ferrari automobile. I. Title.
GV1032.L38A3613   796.7'2'0924 [B]   78-7559
ISBN 0-87938-059-4

2   3   4   5   6   7   8   9   10

Preface

For the record I have chosen from many experiences (for example, sixty races in four years), describing some in detail while leaving others aside, according to the importance they have in my memory, and according to my feelings about them as I look back.

I cannot claim objectivity, because naturally I can only relate subjectively what happened, simply and solely from my own viewpoint.

I have written *My Years With Ferrari* in the frame of mind of a person who sits down to write what he remembers, without worrying about the 'show' or seeking to alter the circumstances in any way.

NIKI LAUDA
October 1977

Editorial collaborator:
HERBERT VÖLKER

English translation by
DIANA MOSLEY

Photo series captions translated by
BERLITZ

Black & white photograph credits: Alois H. Rottensteiner (10), Bernd Schilling (9), Kaszay (4), Bild-Zeitung (2), Austria Wochenschau (1), Roger Benoit (1), Oskar Weissengruber (1)

The publisher gratefully thanks Verlag Orac, Vienna; and William Kimber Co., Ltd., London for their cooperation and generous assistance in the production of this volume.

Contents

PART
ONE

1. Prologue

For weeks the Old Man had been wanting to talk to me and I kept making excuses. Then we arranged to meet on a Wednesday but suddenly this seemed too long to wait.

On Sunday I rang Luca and said, 'Tomorrow. I'll come tomorrow. And anyway I don't want to drive for you any more.'

Luca telephoned on Monday before my flight and offered me what amounted to a blank cheque.

'It's going to be difficult,' I said.

We met at four in the afternoon, in Enzo Ferrari's office; his Modena office, not in Maranello. Present were: the Old Man, his son Piero Lardi, Luca Montezemolo and the accountant. The accountant had an adding machine in front of him, which I didn't like; ugh, I thought, that's unpleasant. Until then he had never appeared. Usually he was on holiday when wages were being discussed, and then they always said: We must wait till we talk to the accountant. This time they had evidently decided to speed things up.

Ferrari opened the discussion. He offered to clear any difficulties away, he offered me privileges, and said money would be no problem.

I said, I'd promised to drive for him as long as he lived. But my feelings had changed, and I asked him to set me free. I don't want to drive for you, I said. The Old Man shouted:

'*Cosa Vuoi*? What do you want?' *Nothing*, said I, that's the point. I don't want anything. I just want to go away.

Ferrari fussed for an hour about what to say to the press, he made me stay so that we could agree on the statement. It had something about mutual gratitude and so forth. It was all one to me. I shook hands with them all round and left. I felt relaxed and happy, as if I'd just fallen in love, or pulled off something terrific. I drove straight to Bologna airport. As I sat in the aeroplane I heard the voice from the control tower: 'You've got a delay of two hours. No more priorities, no more VIP treatment. You left Ferrari, you bastard.'

I replied, 'Have you gone mad? Give me the starting signal. I'm staying anyway in Italy.' 'Okay,' he said, and let me taxi to the runway.

A week later Enzo Ferrari said in an interview, 'Lauda is worse than Judas. He sells himself for thirty sausages to our rivals.'

It wasn't quite like that. He ought to have known my worth.

But I won't quarrel about that with the man many people consider the greatest personality in the history of motor racing. In the years of my career described in this book, Ferrari, the man, his team, his work people, played a dominant role for me – sometimes exciting, sometimes depressing. There is no account to settle up; we are quits. I believe both sides gained from each other; emotional post mortems are pointless.

Naturally Ferrari appears over and over again in this book. But I am telling the story of my professional life, neither more nor less, and there is nothing beyond that to be read into it.

2. Just One of Those Days

I had gastric flu, and went to bed at ten, pretty exhausted. The alarm was set for six, but I woke earlier. A glance out of the window: rain, low clouds, bad flying weather. I woke Helmut, my pilot. Also James Hunt, who was flying with us. We were a hundred kilometres from the race course, on the lake, for peace and quiet. I got everything going. A car takes us to the airport, clouds hide the mountains. The weather is tiresome, because of the flight. We see Colin Chapman's airplane which takes off in visibility nil. We fly our small jet by instruments eastward. Visibility gets worse all the time, down below cars are being driven with their lights on. A worrying flight. We land on the military airfield, people, soldiers, but everything goes like lightning, I climb into the helicopter and away. Rain and people, people, people. Bertl is waiting on the race course with an umbrella, I run to the pits. The surface is so wet that practice is impossible. Confusion, gloom. The warming-up practice is announced. The car is still in the pits, I go to Nosetto and ask what's wrong, in ten minutes the warming-up is due to begin. Don't worry, he says, but I do worry, says I, because I want to use every single minute, the rain has changed everything. I mustn't be nervous, he says.

The mechanics are nervous, they rush hectically around and forget to shut the top of the radiator cap. We only found out at the end of the warming-up, after twenty laps, because when the water level falls the thermometer sensor is left hanging in the air; so you get no warning. We don't know whether the engine has suffered or not. There is no time to change it, we have only an hour and a half, and it would take twice as long. In the Ferrari transporter I lie down and rest and eat a little. Then comes the dreaded moment, I have to go out through gaping crowds. I am angry when I see the photographers putting their heavy gear on the Ferrari, on the wings whose settings have been calculated to the last millimetre. I shout to my mechanics, they must look sharp; get out, get away, everyone. The pressure because of the rain is terrific. Slicks or wet weather tyres is the question that worries everyone. When I look at the other drivers I see they are in the same boat. With slicks on the wet track one can so easily make a mistake, the car has a devil in it, it slides about and there's nothing you can do. All the same I decide for slicks, and get them to set the wings for a dry track.

A good start, I am in the front row, and out in front. At the first corner I notice the brute is not going as it should, and that I have no chance. I might with greater risk go faster, to compensate for the car's disadvantage. But today that's senseless, so I face facts and drive safely. It is ghastly when one after another the cars overtake you, I got further and further behind, until I was tenth. Calm, Roland, calm; something will soon happen. I must just get through this phase. The track, covered in water, is dangerous, the car is handling badly, I am nervous and also furious, because one after another they all pass me. Furious too because of my bad decision : I had believed after five laps it would be dry, and now we'd done twenty. I should have had less wing in front, that would have been better for me.

As the track dries, my car goes better and I can drive

normally; I attack from the back. I see Hunt's car standing
in the pits, and that Andretti is out of the race. I have passed
Scheckter and am already 18 seconds in front of him when
he is also out of the race : a joke, that he skids on the last
wet corner. A gift for me, okay.

Now there's only one in front, and there's not much hope
of catching up with him. Second place is best this time.
Then everything builds up to the verge of pain. The hectic
pace, the sweat, gradually drying and making one cold and
dirty. Then the stupid ceremony, the puffing and blowing,
hands stretched out. In the transport I pull off my overall,
people push me into the corner. From the other side Forghieri
shouts at me, telling me all the mistakes I made. If I had
accelerated in the rain, like Hunt, I should have won, he says.
If I had had the wing set properly, I would have won he
declares. I try to explain, but he won't listen, so I tell him
to go and stuff himself and jump out to get in the helicopter.
Then the television people want me, they say I must come into
their studio. No, I say, I can't; I'm all in. But I go all the
same, and sit down, and then one of the cameras doesn't
work, and I say if you are not ready in three seconds I'm off,
and Frau Dr Kafka is amazed, usually Lauda is so good in
front of the cameras, and now suddenly he's so crazy. It is
serious; the pain threshold has been reached, my head is
swimming, but I pull myself together and say something to
the television, then I run to the helicopter which takes me to
my jet, and as soon as I can fly myself I unwind and become
normal again.

The flight is good, I feel completely relaxed. In Salzburg
the Jaguar is at the airport. I drive to Marlene in the
hospital and describe the race to her, she is happy. My gastric
upset is back again and I rush to the lavatory non-stop. I've
got stomach ache and headache. I drive home, take a shower
and get into bed at eight. I can't sleep, keep waking up,

thinking of this and that. At midnight I take a sleeping pill. I wake at seven, half dead.

3. To make me tough

1972 and 1973 were my crisis years. I had sold myself to March, and then to BRM, borrowed two huge loans, and everything was built on the optimism of a man who plays so high that by normal reckoning he can't win. It can only succeed if something terrific happens.

That at March and BRM nothing terrific was going to happen became obvious after a while. There wasn't enough money, technique or organisation, not enough class.

My cousin Eugen (I call him Jenzy) let me use his Salzburg office as my headquarters. It had become a ritual that I always asked as I came in: 'Has Enzo telephoned?' And Jenzy answered with some joke or other: 'No, not today' or 'Telephone out of order' or something. I didn't really expect Ferrari to telephone but he represented greatness; I must reach him if I was ever to get up out of the mud.

Ferrari was simply the biggest name, the most established firm, so much greater, and more important, and to be taken more seriously than the odd BRM enterprise, in which old Louis Stanley pulled motors and men like rabbits out of a hat, and very often he successfully raised money for the team.

I took it as a new variation on our old jokes, when in summer 1973 Jenzy said: 'Ferrari rang up.'

'Well, well,' said I, 'did he say he'll throw up everything to get the great Lauda?'

But Jenzy was too excited to joke. Monte-so-and-so had telephoned, asking for secrecy and a rendezvous. The name turned out to be Montezemolo, Ferrari's racing team manager, and I met him in August in London. Luca Montezemolo, an important figure in my career : young, tall, elegant, cultured, a lawyer who came from the Agnelli dynasty. He was on his way up in Fiat, and obviously was destined for the very top. Luca is a good man all the same, and that makes everything easier with him.

He said he brought me a proposition from the Commendatore, and asked how much money I wanted. I said a million Austrian schillings a year, and we had terrible trouble turning that into lire, and showed we were greenhorns.

We agreed that after the Austrian Grand Prix I should come into the Ferrari works. I could just as well have come sooner, because after a practice at the Österreichring it was obvious that I couldn't race. Two weeks before I had an accident at the Nürburgring (tyre burst at 250, a 400 m slide down the slope) and broke my right arm; the pain was still severe.

I met Montezemolo at a motor road exit, he drove me to Maranello and to the Ferrari test track at Fiorano. There I saw exactly what the Viennese journalist Helmut Zwickl later described thus : 'Ferrari, compared with all the other Formula I teams is like NASA, the American space project, compared with a club to promote the ascent of the Drachen.' Yes, I was still under contract to climb the Drachen, and suddenly I saw all the technical marvels : a private race track with automatic time-keeping, with closed circuit television and computers. A comparably vast team of fitters, engineers, administrators. I couldn't imagine how such a set-up could fail to win. Okay, Ferrari had had no success for some years, but it was obvious to me that this potential was unequalled, and something must be made of it. That afternoon Enzo Ferrari came to the test track, kindly, avuncular, nice. Luca translated: would I like to drive? I said yes. True, BRM had an option on me for next year, but I signed at once for Ferrari and thought I could easily get out of the other thing. All the same I had endless trouble with BRM later. The Marlboro lawyers assured me, however, that what I had done was quite in order.

I began my job with Ferrari in late Autumn 1973. Testing, testing, and again testing. The car to begin with was unbelievably hard to drive, and became step by step better. With Mauro Forghieri there was not much contact but no difficulties either. Even with my partner Clay Regazzoni everything was okay. We were never real friends, but I valued him. He is so perfectly the type of racing driver: women; small, rough and stocky; moustache. He is a typical cinema champion, such as people sometimes think of as being the real thing. He is still one of the old guard drivers. Nonsense, of course; Clay just happens to look that way by chance.

In the 1974 season it sometimes looked as if I were already on top. And so I was in many ways. I had no more money worries, I had got myself out of the jungle. The whole season was spent learning – among other things I learnt how to lose, not ordinary losing, but the hardest kind. For the first time I was first in practice, for the first time I dominated a race (South Africa), then something went wrong four laps from the finish. Again fastest in practice, again I dominated the race (Monaco) and again the same problem at the identical moment, a defect which had been examined and passed as put right. I learnt how to win and I learnt from my mistakes, and I realized that it is a curious fact that a lot of little things can add up to a great zero.

Nürburgring: the mechanics' mistake, when instead of

pushing the car through all the dirt and debris between the garage and the pits on wet weather tyres they had already fitted my race tyres. The right hand front tyre was damaged and had to be changed, I knew how careful I must be until its 'run in'. Then bad luck : it drizzled during the warming-up lap and we drove so slowly that the new tyre was not run in at all. We had problems with the shock absorbers; should we change them? The first mistake : I make a bad start. The second mistake : I am too impatient; I don't want Regazzoni to get ahead – if he gets away right from the start I shall never catch him up, so I must stay with him, and Scheckter is preventing me, he's between me and Rega. Third mistake : I want to pass Scheckter immediately. At that moment the combination of all the mistakes : the drizzle on the warming up lap, my impatience, my bad start and the cold tyre all add up to a great flop : as I jam on the brakes the car swerves to the right into Scheckter's car, the Ferrari jumps over Scheckter's wheels up in the air.

This was the worst of a whole series of accidents that season, I never got within reach of my goal. Towards the end I had lost my chance of the world championship and had to support Regazzoni who was just as unlucky. I remember a television interview, I said : 'This year I wasn't ready to become world champion. If I have a good season next year, I shall know the reason for it all : to make me tough and ready for great things.'

Great things came with a rush. 1975 was the unbelievable year when we and the Ferrari 31ST held the entire racing world in our grasp. We had the most modern and developed construction, we had as many test kilometres behind us as all the other teams combined, as we all agreed at the beginning of the European season. Out of eleven races I started nine in pole position, won five times and with almost twenty points lead was world champion. It was the reward for all our work for the last eighteen months; we got back what we gave in headaches, money and work. We changed the face of Grand Prix racing, we woke up the Drachen climbers, gave an example of technical development and precision work through the intensive testing such as had never before existed in motor racing. I believe we dragged all those who are now making such cleverly designed and splendid cars along with us, and laid the foundations for the tremendous spring forward that has made Formula I into the technical business we know today.

At the same time we created a Ferrari crisis, because it could never be bettered, and the tremendous successes brought new problems with them. Once my team manager went so far as to say before a race that I must let the others win 'because you've already won too often.'

Ferrari, the racing team, is unique in the world, and it has unique problems too. They begin with the myth of the 80 year old Commendatore, who is such a sacred figure for the Italians that they go flat on their faces before him. When I say '*Ciao,* Enzo' bystanders are always shocked, because hardly anyone calls him anything but President, or Commendatore, or even '*Ingegnere*'. His people are so much in awe of this monumental patriarch that it is a source of misunderstandings and mistaken decisions. They would rather please the Old Man by telling him something nice (untrue) instead of something less nice (true). Helmet Zwickl gave a hundred per cent correct example of this attitude in *Autorevue* in spring 1977 when he wrote :

A small telephone box at Silverstone. Rude words scribbled on the walls, in English. Near me stood a genius with spectacles and handwritten notes on a bit of paper. While in my left ear the operator kept saying 'Sorry for the delay' in our call to Maranello, the genius began changing the lap times on the paper with his ballpoint pen. He took a tenth of a second off Lauda's time. That's a lot in Formula I. And he added something to Andretti's.

My left ear heard, 'Sorry, sorry', my right ear could hardly believe what it heard : 'There, that looks better.'

What looks better?

The whole team, travel expenses, raw ham, spaghetti and parmesan cheese, the lot, and a red racing car had gone to Silverstone.

The whole Ferrari team was going to please the old Commendatore, who came to the telephone himself a few moments later.

Mauro Forghieri, the genius near me in the telephone box, had thought up something else.

The trick with the times?

The false bottom belongs to Ferrari like the twelve cylinder motor. The self-deception belongs to Ferrari like the Agip fuel. No, the trick was an old one. But the front axle was new. Even Lauda stood better now, if such a thing were possible. Nikolaus was leading at this point in the world championship. One couldn't do better with such a rotten car as Ferrari.

To be leader in the world championship, that was the top.

'Good, my boy,' Enzo Ferrari will have said. 'Nothing is good,' I hear Lauda say. 'It's all shit.'

I am not much of a hand at 'historical merit' and the cult of legends. For me, Enzo Ferrari was just the Chief of my racing team, and I always treated him with respect, but straightforwardly. When I wanted to talk with him I knocked on his door and went in, whereas even for his closest colleagues the ritual is to ask for an interview. The show is a bit terrifying I must admit : the empty room painted dark blue, the great portrait of his dead son, usually with candles burning in front of it, and at the writing table the aged President. If you feel a bit upset by all this, you feel more upset still on the way out, impressed by so much quiet grandeur. If you talk to him properly, all goes normally; the Old Man is not only a personality but also a good and kindly man, who lives up to his great reputation. Therefore in all my years with Ferrari I never had a single problem with him in direct approach, ever. The problems always began when I got outside and his 'advisers' got going.

In order to be a driver for Ferrari you need political strength within the Chief's inner circle. What is needed is a man who will brief the Commendatore on the drivers, the team, the community success and everything else, and make the right suggestions. His lobby is so important because the Old Man never goes to a race. He gets his information about every detail, he demands all the technical data on practices and training, he has to know all about the water temperature as well as tyre wear and tear.

The man who gives him this information is naturally in a strong position to influence his decisions, because he can present the facts in such and such a way. If a wrong decision is made, they often stick to it. It's a bit too much to expect a Patriarch to make a 180 degree change, it's just not on. In the first two years I had this political strength through Luca Montezemolo, in the circle closest to the President. Luca had had power by reason of his birth (in 1947), but later he grew into it. Despite his youth he always had his entry to the Old Man, and he trusted me. After a time he got the idea that my 'feeling' was right, and he was my right hand with the President.

What were the decisions? To do with priorities in technical development, test times, test tracks, concentration of the potential (for example, should a third driver start?) and in all these questions the balance (for example between the authorities and safety precautions).

Montezemolo was big enough to hold the ring between me and Mauro Forghieri. Mauro was one of the chief reasons why I left Ferrari, but I must admit there is a lot to be said for him. He is a good chap, even more, and he's a techincal genius. Unfortunately he is also crazy. He makes snap decisions, ignores realities, insists he is right, and then you can't argue with him. He has got the psychological finesse of a sand viper. One important thing he has never understood in his life: that you must persuade a man, and having persuaded him you must not endlessly change your mind. When the Ferrari went well and all was perfect, he considered me a very good driver, perhaps the best. When things went wrong, I was an idiot, I must see how marvellously Reutemann or Andretti or Brambilla drove. The slightest accident he always blames on the driver. He won't admit that I am in a certain class always (apart from small details sometimes, but this is not a case of small details). Instead of trying to work together on the various problems which arise, he imagines one is the enemy. The driver, especially the driver with technical knowledge, needs a go-between for himself and Forghieri, otherwise the wear and tear is too much for both sides. As I said before, I consider Mauro Forghieri is a technical genius, but it's just too difficult to live with him.

4. World Champion

Summer 1975, that incomparable late summer, Lauda the computer, Lauda the technician, Lauda the calculator, Lauda the cool customer, is almost World Champion. But the computer is in love. 'Action Ibiza', we manage it several times in those weeks, secret journeys for which we need a discreet and silent pilot, Marlene and I. I have avoided all publicity and no journalist has an inkling of our trips. They are the most beautiful days of my life.

Then Monza, and the World Champion title. The consequence : my professional goal has been reached, and next year I shall earn more money. No festivities, except little ones, just the two of us. A few quarrels with friends about it, but honours bore me, it's not for them that I have become World Champion. The official prize from the sport authorities, a dinner service for twelve, soon finds another good home. What could I do with these giant dishes? I felt like a head waiter with them : 'More fish, my lord?'

I revise my market value, naturally. Every public creature has its market value. Mine goes up thirty per cent. Otherwise nothing was changed in my life as a result of being world champion; absolutely nothing. One day on Ibiza gives me more than all the honours put together. My know-how has reached the summit of effort, and surpassed it. Any further increase of the Star image is nothing but a nuisance. One must arrange one's life in such a way as to be very careful that even private life shall not become public. This was particularly difficult during the weeks I spent in a Salzburg hotel. I had moved out of the house I shared with Mariella Reisinghaus; my own house is not yet ready. I deny everything. Marlene Knaus? Yes, I know her. Nothing more. I don't want to be a magazine hero. I want to be known for my driving, not as a society man or a lover or God knows what. At Ferrari's Forghieri makes an about-turn and our test programme for the USA race goes by the board. Okay we are already World Champion, but we must keep up the pressure or else next year we shall fall behind. Forghieri will come to the race but not for the practice. Everything is bust, the whole programme, the continuity.

Forghieri tells everyone how fantastic the new Ferrari will be, though only a wooden model exists so far. The team is lulled to sleep with success, and by degrees the whole technical advance is lost.

The loss of Luca Montezemolo is a great blow to me. Of course it's his career; he cannot stay forever with Ferrari, at 28 he must get back into the mainstream of power and advancement at Fiat; but I always knew that I needed him in the power struggle at Ferrari's, and he had promised to uphold me. I needed him badly just two weeks after he left : he had to enthuse the Old Man, make the row of the century, stop the carelessness, bring Forghieri into line.

The Old Man is furious with Forghieri, wants to put him in cold storage, as he calls it.

I won at Watkins Glen, the last race, a victory for diligent attention to detail.

5. Water Polo

Montezemolo's career lift carried him up through the press department to be public relations chief to the Fiat company. This made him also head of all the racing activities of the group; therefore he was still a weapon I could use. Nevertheless we needed a new team manager for the 1976 season at Ferrari's. 'Manager' is perhaps too much to say, because in any case the chief and the manager was always Enzo Ferrari, no matter how much he officially retired from the firm. The racing stable is his personal hobby until death, so much is certain, and there is nobody who would disturb that in the slightest. The most important job for a Ferrari team manager is therefore giving objective information to the Old Man, and influencing his opinion. There are very few men who even have the right background to be so much as considered for such a job and fewer still who are up to it. Montezemolo was naturally anxious that his successor should be the right person to understand the Old Man and get his confidence, and he spoke to me about it. We agreed upon Danieli Audetto, at that time manager of the Lancia rally team. He belonged to the Fiat family, was expert in the sport and made a good impression. I met him in December 1975 in Rome and described the job, he behaved sensibly.

It was obvious to me that the job was delicate. On the one hand we were already at the very top, as World

Champions, on the other he was torn between his natural ambition to make his own decisions and the fact that Regazzoni and I had the enormous advantage of experience and information. He could be team leader, but if he is to give the orders he must make the right decisions; right for me, for the team, for success. If he makes a wrong decision he becomes my opponent. Psychologically I built Audetto up, gave him honest public support. Not for nothing is water polo an Italian expression to describe business life : the fouls are done with the feet under the water where the umpire cannot see them.

At the beginning all went well. We had very different ideas about social life, but that didn't matter. Audetto loves society, elegant dinner parties are terribly important to him, and he was very disappointed when he saw that I was not the right partner for his fashionable outings. Slowly he realized – mostly through the Italian press, who treated him with great respect – what an unbelievably important job it is to be racing team leader for Ferrari's; he was quite overcome by his own importance.

I had won in Brazil and South Africa and had a good lead in the world championship when we arrived at Long Beach. Audetto was naturally closer to Regazzoni than he was to me, partly because they spoke the same language but also because of Clay's more enthusiastic social life. In any case Audetto came up with the idea that this time Regazzoni must be allowed to win. 'Are you mad?' I asked him. 'These points will be needed for me to win the world championship.'

He made a gesture as though to say the world championship was already in the bag. However, I made it clear to him that he must put any such idea right out of his head. As long as the world championship is not decided each man must drive for himself. All the same Danieli Audetto got his wish at Long Beach : a double win for Ferrrari, Regazzoni in front of

Lauda. This was nothing to do with a pre-arranged plan; it was because my car had problems. But he himself was naturally enormously pleased and proudly walked about more importantly than ever. Ferrari in first (me) and third (Rega) places for the world championship – what a splendid success.

My own position was splendid, but from now on my life changed. One among many outward signs of this was that I got married.

6. Marlene

The wedding at the Wiener Neustadt registry office was a total success; not one single journalist, only the necessary two witnesses, one of whom brought me a tie so that I could look smart for the ceremony. It was two weeks before there was anything in the newspapers.

The marriage was the logical conclusion of the happy days on Ibiza and the end of my near-marriage with Mariella Reininghaus.

I had been seven years with Mariella and was almost certain that one of these days we should get married. Mariella was very disciplined, quiet, clever, thoughtful, with endless patience. During test driving and practice she could sit for hours on a heap of tyres without moving or speaking – she was good at Yoga. If I came by once an hour and gave her a kiss she was perfectly satisfied. Her self-control was sometimes almost uncanny. She had great influence over me, and tried to have even more. Up to a point I was glad to let this happen, everything to do with my house, the building of which she almost entirely took over (we were living then in a little town flat in Salzburg).

When it became obvious that I should probably be World Champion in 1975 she began to make plans for me to give up driving. Become World Champion, then finish with it.

Family, a decent job, that was her line, and she pushed it hard. I had no desire at the age of 26 to retire, even though age had little to do with it. I simply didn't want to do it and I dreaded the endless arguments which would ensue if in fact I stayed in racing after becoming World Champion. We quarrelled more and more often, and I went away more in the summer of 1975 – I had to have a change.

Then I met Marlene Knaus. She was the girl friend of Curt Jürgens and as such was hostess at a party in Salzburg. She spoke to me; a spark flew between us. Two rendezvous, a few visits to the hospital (she had pneumonia), a little outing from the hospital, 'Action Ibiza', and everything was clear to me. I moved out of the flat.

One Sunday my architect rang up and said he had seen in the paper that I had left Mariella. 'That's a dirty trick,' said he, 'I wanted to build the house for you and Fräulein Reininghaus.' He declared he would not finish the house, and furthermore he was insulted because I called his staircase 'bloody awful'. He had planned a staircase with transparent plastic banisters, ultra modern, but it looked like the Innsbruck branch of the *Raiffeisenkasse*. True, I had never bothered about the house, except to give my opinion on the staircase, and to lay down one or two important points. In front I wanted to be able to see the Fuschl lake, and at the back, where I should sleep, the forest. And there must be the swimming pool. The garage must take four cars, and the baths must be sunk in the floor. Everything else was done between Mariella and the architect, and I drove straight out there to have a look and see what was going on. I found nothing but concrete and iron. The idea was modern techniques, Lauda – racing cars – iron – concrete. The garage was designed so low that a Range Rover wouldn't have got in; probably the architect imagined Lauda drove nothing but racing Ferraris. Anyway I was appalled, and immediately got

Marlene's brother Tilly going. He is a painter, with taste, and he knows what's what. He got much of the iron replaced with wood, and a lot of the concrete covered in wood, and I was finally very pleased with the house. Marlene and I moved in a few weeks after our wedding, in New Year 1976. At the time of the Monaco Grand Prix Marlene lost a baby.

Marlene is just the opposite of me. I am reserved, thorough and concentrated on the line I take. Marlene makes life cheerful and gay, hers and mine. She is relaxed in a way that I have never known before, either in my family or with Mariella. She knows nothing about motor racing, and I soon began to think that it's a good idea. She comes with me to many races, but only as my companion, without any other function. She hasn't got a stop-watch, doesn't write down the lap times, none of that amuses her and she is quite unlike all the women who are always around, getting into the act, every day with smarter clothes and with their stop-watches at the ready. It is lovely that she hasn't been drawn into motor racing, she is only there for me, not for the sport.

She leaves me my freedom, which I like, and doesn't influence me. She never clings; if she asks, 'Coming to eat?' and I say no, she doesn't ask whether I am taking her with me. She knows that if I wanted her to come I should say so. And I rather like going alone to the airport canteen, for example. In spite of her being so relaxed I know how anxious she is when she comes to my races. Before the start she is all in, I know it from her movements, the way she creeps around like a whipped dog. The Nürburgring accident had a lot to do with this. When girls and women accompany a racing driver they get a lot of his optimism, the feeling that 'nothing can go wrong'. And when it does happen, and they see you lying there, their eyes are opened. They never feel the same again about motor racing, they never have that unworried attitude, they think and they see things which formerly didn't

31

exist for them. That is why I won't take her to all the Grands Prix, in the end it's just too much of a worry for her.

Our house is about ten kilometres from Salzburg in the direction of the Fuschl lake, and I am grateful to anyone who doesn't come visiting, because it has become the favourite outing of crowds of tourists who want to stare at Lauda. I have no patience with people who disturb me in this way. I quite realize that as a public animal I have my duty to the public, but I stick to the point of view that this ends at my own private property. I want peace and quiet there, and nothing else, and my house gives it to me. It turned out rather big and when I am alone there I don't know where to go, but on the whole the size is right. I only wanted to build once in my life, it is a house for always. I shall always stay in Austria, the country I like best.

7. Suddenly, Chaos

I had borrowed a tractor from Enzinger-Wastl, to work on the bank by the swimming pool. The thing tipped over and buried me underneath it.

If I had been sitting in it in the ordinary way I should have been killed, but I had the luck to fall between the caterpillar wheels so that I didn't get the whole weight on me, also the earth was fairly soft so that my head was buried in a cushion.

All the same, my whole right side is done for, broken ribs, blood everywhere, I can't get up without help. The chances of being ready for the Spanish Grand Prix in a fortnight are minimal.

Lauda runs himself over with a tractor, what a sensation! Ferrari immediately sends Santi Ghedini, as chauffeur, bodyguard, press chief, telephonist. He runs out of the house with a broom to chase the journalists away. At the Friesacher in Anif four Italian newspapermen are staying and they ring up every few minutes. In the mountain opposite a giant telephoto lens is set up.

Down below they all get going. Sabbatini, the pope of the magazine *Autosprint,* urges on the Old Man to put Flammini in my car. Italians must stick together, a chance for Flammini and so forth. Such a silly idea, half way through the season to have a completely inexperienced driver in Formula I! Some Italians are so fanatical, that no Italian is bad or inexperienced enough not to be put forward as an alternative. Regazzoni, who has at least got an Italian name, has a renaissance, while Audetto is suddenly emperor because he was the one who 'made' Rega win again. Audetto sent a message, I must spare myself and stay in bed. He was for ever ringing up at the office to speak to me, as though my bed was there; he never got my private number although everyone at Ferrari's knew it, and unfortunately a few journalists knew it too. I told one of them that Italian racing drivers were good for nothing but driving round the church tower, and it was in the *Gazetta dello Sport* next day. All Italy howled with rage, but I didn't care. In my position I had to say something tough.

A fascinating situation : yesterday a hero, as soon as I was lying on my back I'd had my chips. One of the main reasons for the chaos and muddle was that the Old Man and his people take what they see in the papers so terribly seriously. If they didn't have a heart attack over every false rumour everything would be a lot easier. If Ferrari is criticized telegrams fly to and fro, there are reports and denials, and great excitement, and all that comes through to the drivers. I soon twigged how things are for a foreign Ferrari driver in Italy. In part of the press you have no hope; you can drive like a god, say nothing but nice things in Italian and always eat spaghetti, it doesn't do the slightest good, you are still a swine according to them. Therefore I concentrated on a few sensible journalists and gave them information and the others, the enemies, the drivellers, the misquoters, the unteachables, I ignored.

When Montezemolo wanted to speak to me about the 'Flammini for Spain' idea, I said : 'If you have nothing against it, and if it doesn't interfere with your plans, it would be very kind if you would let *me* drive in Spain. I shall go for practice and then we'll see, and if that doesn't suit you you can go and stuff yourselves. And perhaps you could call a halt to all this chaos, because everyone can see the world championship disappearing.'

The doctor said it would take six weeks to get better. When I breathe in and out it still goes tuck tuck tuck, but after a fortnight the cracked ribs would heal, and then we can see better. A fortnight, that's exactly when the Spanish Grand Prix takes place. I can do nothing, nothing to help, I can only lie as quietly as possible and breathe as decently as possible.

Thank God there are also nice fellows. John Hogan, the sport chief at Marlboro, sent me a telegram :

WORLD LAWN MOWER CHAMPION SORRY TO HEAR THAT YOU LOST CONTROL MAYBE MODEL WITH REDUCED POWER WOULD DO BETTER IN FUTURE — CSI SERIOUSLY CONSIDERING ADAPT-ING NEW FORMULA FOR NEXT SEASON — MANDATORY REQUIREMENTS WILL BE ROLLOVER BAR, SEATBELTS EXPERIENCED DRIVER AND POWER LIMITED TO 10 HORSE-POWER — ALL SWIMMING POOLS AND POOL-SIDE TREES TO BE SURROUNDED WITH ARMCO — SEE YOU ON POLE IN SPAIN — HOGAN.

It did me good in the midst of chaos to get this telegram.

The miracle : Willy Dungl. A masseur and healer of genius — at any rate judging by the results in my case.

After two long painful weeks, many Dungl tricks and hard clenching of teeth, I went to Spain and was second behind Hunt. Then first, when they disqualified him (because his McLaren was too wide), then again second, when they changed their minds again. As usual, the chaos had been defeated.

Then began the phenomenon of boredom : people were fed up with Lauda, I won too often and I was to blame that the sport was becoming a bore. I simply refused to discuss such nonsense – who would benefit if the best allowed the second best to win? Nevertheless at the next race, at Zolder in Belgium, I was confronted once again by our famous team manager. When I was first and Regazzoni second in practice, Audetto began his thesis, which in my opinion could only be justified if there were really tremendous tactical reasons, such as a decisive lead in the world championship. Otherwise it is nonsense, and cheating the public. Audetto said in any case I must stay second, if Clay made the best start. In that case he would hold out a notice board for me, orders from the pits, with plus and minus and all that crap. Good old Audetto had a sort of new-boy complex and thought he must be a great team leader with a great strategy. I told him he could hang out any notice board he liked, yellow, green or red, with plus and minus and double minus, I shouldn't look at it. And that's what happened, and I won the race. Audetto had by now reached the limit as far as I went. One of the two of us would have to leave at the end of the season, that much was obvious.

I have got the lap chart of the Monaco race course in front of me. The lines, which show the position of the car in each of the 78 laps have less point than anywhere else, because overtaking is so difficult and therefore there's not so much change of position. I myself had a straight run, I started from pole and was first at the finish. One of those victories which are a bit of a bore : once again first from beginning to end, said the reports.

A lovely start, I am in front. One little mistake : not Regazzoni but Peterson is right behind me; he may put on the pressure but for the moment there's no danger. Since they made the second chicane Monaco is harder than ever, the breaking – halting – accelerating has become so quick that it demands terrific concentration. I drew away from Ronnie, but then he closed up again, he looms bigger and bigger in my mirror. At the harbour chicane there's oil on the track. One must anyway go slower because there's a McLaren there, Hunt's car apparently with motor trouble. Because of this the ideal line – from the outside right into the left hand corner – is blocked, you have to go left past the car. In the next lap the McLaren is far behind. I think about the oil on the last lap, and that where the car stood there must now be more oil. Therefore I already abandon the ideal line and stay on the left, see a little oil, but get the car more or less clean through. I look in the mirror, no Peterson, a nice surprise.

The worry is no less, because my hands and the cramped neck muscles hurt. I concentrate with all that is in me, but it becomes more and more difficult to do what must be done. About fifteen laps before the end I come round by the Casino and go into second instead of third.

The motor screeches, I quickly correct it before something awful happens. It is a shock to my whole body. Bloody fool, look out, pull yourself together! Fury with myself gives me strength to overcome my exhaustion.

The brief moment of joy : the chequered flag, victory. With that, the capacity to be pleased with oneself is exhausted. During the victory lap I must wave, and look in the mirror in case somebody wants to overtake. Everything overwhelms me together : the noise, the people, the pushing and shoving and slapping on the back; wreaths, cups, anthems, princes, microphones; hurry away, only get away, a car is organized, then the helicopter, then the 'Golden Eagle'. Marlene has lost her baby, she needs me and I need her. And I'm much too tired, too emptied, to be pleased; I've no strength left for that. But waking next morning is lovely : hey, you won! Then it all begins again, telephone, Marlene, fixtures. Joy over the victory has simply no chance to get through.

I was third in Sweden, had engine failure in France and won in England, only after James Hunt was disqualified.

8. Talk Show

Two days after Brands Hatch there's an interview with the Old Man in the *Corriere della Sera*. He said that since I'd gone crazy about flying I didn't bother enough about the car, I neglected my work, and was to blame for the last gear transmission defect, and so on.

One day later I see him: 'So, now say all that to my face! Come on: when have I been late, what have I missed? Tell me of one single day which I have missed practice, or one single action where I have let myself down.' I pinned him down and finally it all added up to nothing. The whole fuss was just an example of the way irrational fiascos can be built up out of gossip.

The Italian newspapers naturally want to blow the business up, they telephone to ask, have I read that the Commendatore has said this and that, are you pleased about it, what do you say to that? I take no interest in this latest example of chaos and I play it cool. Okay, the Commendatore has given his opinion. I am not going to argue with him. I say nothing.

Then the negotiations about the renewal of the contract. I sit with the Old Man and his son, Piero Lardi, in the back room of the Cavallino Restaurant, opposite the factory at Maranello. My Italian is adequate but in these negotiations Lardi translates Italian/English. He would like me to stay on in 1977, says the Old Man, what would I need for that?

'A team with two drivers, not three,' say I, 'because three would be too much for the capacity of the technicians and mechanics. And for second driver I should like Regazzoni again.'

That will be difficult, says the Old Man, I want to suspend him. The talk goes to and fro and I insist over and over again that for me it would be fine if Regazzoni stayed on.

Then he asked, what about money? How much do I want? I name the sum in schillings, so and so many million schillings. He says not a word, gets up, goes to the telephone, rings the accountant Della Casa and asks him : How much is so and so many million schillings? He waits for the answer, puts down the receiver, comes back and sits facing me, very quietly. THEN HE STARTS TO SHOUT, he bawls me out as never before : Confound your insolent cheek, never heard of such swinish behaviour, you must have gone mad, there's no point in further discussion, we go our separate ways, and when he pauses for breath Piero quickly translates the last curse. A translator is a useful go-between for these sort of negotiations, the swear words can be slightly toned down.

I say to Piero, please tell him, as we are going different ways I should like to fly home, but Piero says I should stay where I was, and it goes back and forth until finally I say Ferrari should make an offer.

No, says the Old Man, he cannot make an offer because he only wants contented drivers in his racing team, and his offer couldn't make me contented.

Very well, then I can really go home, because if my offer is unacceptable and you make no counter proposal, that's the end.

At last he makes his offer, a good quarter below what I demanded, and changed into lire. I get angry and tell Piero to tell him that his team manager has already offered me a few million lire more than that. My anger is real; I have no respect for him because we are equal partners. He wants to buy my achievement and it costs such and such.

'What, is that true about Audetto?' shouts the Old Man.

Yes, I say, call him in and ask him. He gets Audetto in and asks him if he offered such a sum of money? Yes, says Audetto, I proposed so and so much.

Then Ferrari says to me, okay, if such a madman among my employees offers so much I give in, and he says to Audetto, 'We'll talk later' and lets him go. But this is my last offer, he shouts at me, he roars like a bull.

To show good-will I take off a percentage, quite calmly. Then he calms down and says I'm shameless, it's madness, it's too much for his nerves and do I want to kill him, so then I say to Piero:

'Tell him, Ferrari would never have been World Champion but for me.'

Piero: 'I can't translate that, that I won't.'

I tell him not to be a coward, he must translate it and quickly too, and Piero pulls himself together and translates it, red in the face. Then the Old Man begins to roar again, and so it goes on for about an hour, until he asks how much I want, and I go down another four per cent, my final proposition.

Then he says: *Okay, Ebreo* – okay, you Jew, but of course he can say what he likes, it's in the price he pays. Next minute he is as charming and nice, a delightful old gentleman, pleasant to talk to, as one could imagine. I have seen and heard the greatest talk show of my life.

There was a lot of talk about Clay Regazzoni, the Old Man is furious with him, because Clay had bashed into the guard rails at Monaco and was to blame for a collision with me at Brands Hatch. Right after the start he braked too late on Paddock Corner and wanted to pass me on the inside, which was simply impossible. Then he rammed my back wheel, which I could have survived except that his car was across the track so that two other cars ran into it.

Clay tried to put the blame on me, but that was ridiculous, as I told him : 'It's enough, when you're ten centimetres behind – whoever gets to the corner to have let the madman pass me must remember that the corner had adverse camber, so that if I had swerved left and not kept my line I should have found myself over the rails and in the field.' I don't know whether Clay accepted that and I don't care; we didn't quarrel about it.

Anyway, Clay was in disgrace. And the Old Man got excited over it and said Clay must behave properly; what cheek, he said. Then the Old Man told what according to him was the dirtiest trick of all, when he was driving to Modena he saw women wearing Clay Regazzoni jeans, and he furiously described what those jeans were like. They had the *cavallo* on the behind, the horse on their arses, the rearing horse of the Ferrari coat of arms. The Old Man was furious : 'What cheek, what insolence, the fellow sells his pants with the Ferrari horse on the bottom !'

Clay is there at luncheon, he stays silent. Only when the Old Man accuses him of complaining against Ferrari in public Rega murmured : 'That's not true.' Then Ferrari told him he could go to Ghozzi(the Ferrari press man) and see the ten pages of newspaper cuttings. The old problem : Ferrari and the newspapers.

Then there was a discussion between Ferrari, Lardi, Forghieri and Audetto about Regazzoni's fate. The Old Man was so furious that he even wanted to stop him going to the Nürburgring. The decision however was for Clay : he could go on driving, but 'must behave himself properly'.

9. 1st August 1976

Nürburgring: I was under fire because I had complained of the danger. Some of them tried to laugh at me for being a coward, others put forward the wisdom of the old timers (Huschke von Hanstein: 'I drove there forty years ago') basically everyone tried to be clever, whether or no. Coward or not, it helps nobody to make motor racing a series of murderous accidents. If two people are killed in every race, who benefits? Even with all the modern safety devices there will always be accidents and deaths which make people ask whether such a sport is admissible. Therefore it is mad to increase the already enormous risks, by driving on unsafe race tracks. And the Nürburgring is the most unsafe of the lot, simply because it is so long that at most points on the way the ambulances and firefighters are so far off that they take too long to get to the scene of the accident, and this may result in death.

Nürburgring means nothing particular to me, and in the beginning I even loved the Ring, because I was the ideal type of driver for it. A race track which I could work on, in every detail, getting ever more perfect; I was good on the Ring because I knew it so well. Before I first raced there – in Formula V – I practised for a whole week. I have driven in every sort of race on the Ring, even the 24 hour marathon, and I have never had anything against it.

This was because I didn't worry about safety. I just accepted, along with the 'normal' danger of racing driving, the additional, unnecessary danger, without thinking about it. I must try to pinpoint the moment when I awoke to the danger. It must have been in Formula I. Naturally I had already been confronted with accidents where men were killed, but they didn't get under my skin, because there was always the question whether the man himself hadn't made a mistake. Perhaps he'd drunk too much the night before, and lost concentration; or perhaps he was really a bad driver who was not fitted by nature for our sport.

That was the way I thought. It only changed when I got into world class, and saw my colleagues die, men whose expertise I could judge. When you constantly live among men who don't make mistakes but who are nonetheless killed, the question takes on a new dimension. You have to think it through, you can no longer push it to one side. The absurd fire extinguishers when Roger Williamson died, about right for putting out a curtain that had caught fire. The barriers in South Africa which broke when Peter Revson hit them; the beheading of Helmut Koinigg at Watkins Glen. To be confronted by all this and just go on in the old way you would have to be an idiot. And since I woke up, I insist upon fighting the *unnecessary* dangers of motor racing, whether at Nürburgring or Mosport or in Fuji.

In the 1976 situation at Nürburgring I accepted the decision of the majority of the drivers, who illogically one last time were ready to start on the Ring – some wanting to seem brave, others simply too stupid to know what they were doing. And I was also illogical, and satisfied with the thought that it was for the last time.

*

Drizzle, a shower, autumn chill, wretchedness, the start put off a few times, various rumours about the state of the track. One thing certain : it was mostly soaking wet. Therefore wet weather tyres. I was in the front row but made a bad start. Because the track was wet I started in second gear, but I accelerated too much. The wheels rotated too fast, which is even worse in second gear. With a higher gear you practically stop still if the wheels start to spin. That's what happened to me. A normal first lap, skidding but otherwise okay, I was lying ninth. As it got more and more dry I went into the pits for a tyre change. A good quick change —

I hear a rattle, we are landing somewhere : helicopter, I'm in a helicopter.

I lie in bed and think it will soon be all over. I am tired, and want to go to sleep and know nothing more. All over me there are tubes going in and out. I hear voices, see a movement, feel giddy, then I think I mustn't, mustn't, mustn't and I cling to the voice as if to a rope, because as long as I can hear voices I am still alive, and I fight and fight and won't give in, and then I suddenly understand a word : FITTIPALDI and I recognize a voice, the voice of Grajales, Fittipaldi's doctor, I recognize the way he speaks. The fact that I knew his name rouses me; I am conscious, and I know I want to live.

I hear Marlene's voice. I can't see her, I can't speak but I can hear her, which cranks me up to think once more. I understand my situation : accident, hospital, lungs.

I can develop the will to understand – without being able to see, or speak, or move. I understand that my lungs have got to be pumped out, and that it's important, and that it will hurt; that I must help as much as I can; I am ready to try; the pain is cruel.

I am bandaged, blind and dumb. A man appears; I understand it's the priest. He speaks in Latin, it sounds like a judgement. You can die from an extreme unction like that just as you can die from shock. The priest says nothing kind, never mentions the possibility that I might recover.

On the fourth day I understand that my blood-count and lungs are so much better that I shall live.

My memory goes only so far as the stop in the pits, and then a moment in the helicopter, and then the wish to be unconscious in the hospital and the first awakening of the desire to live when I recognized Dr Grajales' voice. Nevertheless in between those times I thought, and even spoke. I learnt that in the helicopter Daniele Audetto found out from me where the key of my car was, and I told him the Bilstein man Hugo Emde had it. All this happened during one of the memory gaps.

I have of course seen films and TV video pictures of the accident dozens of times. I am driving down the Bergwerk, take the left turn at kilometre 10.6, and touch the apex at the concrete kerb. The car breaks away at the back and I put on opposite lock and drift – quite normally, nothing too dramatic. Speed : a bit more than 200 km an hour. Suddenly the car moves to the right, a much more violent movement than would be caused by a steering wheel movement and crashes through the catchfencing, bounces against the embankment and is hurled back so that the tank breaks away. At the same time a pole knocked my helmet off. The Ferrari stands right across the track, Brett Lunger's car crashes into it and sends it 100 metres further. Merzario, Lunger, Edwards and Ertl save my life, by pulling me out of the burning wreck. Most marvellous of all was what Arturo Merzario did; he rushed straight into the flames and managed to get my safety belt undone. His action changed nothing in his attitude to me; he couldn't stand me before, and had often attacked me in the Italian press, and afterwards he did the same. He was a completely selfless saviour. He pulled out a fellow he really disliked.

The burns on my face, head and hands would not have been mortally dangerous; it was the harm done to lungs and blood (through breathing in the fumes of burning petrol) that was.

Intensive care unit in Mannheim : On the fourth day they took the tubes out and for the first time I could speak. Visitors : Marlene, and my relations, all in green, green coats, green caps. I say, 'What have you got on?' They were special sterilized clothes, and they'd been through a sterilizer. Inside the temperature was 30 C. Because of my burns and the special danger of infection they have put me in the intensive care unit in a special little room.

On Thursday they gave me a looking glass. I had to press my eyelids up in order to see clearly. My head is swollen to three times its normal size, it sits like a great melon on my shoulders. Neck and nose are hidden in the swelling. It gives you a bit of a shock to see yourself like that. 800 C, says the nurse, that's what happens in a temperature of 800 C.

The first real success is when I walk a few steps, helped by the nurse. Poor people, I thought, they see nothing here but ghastly accidents. One man had his car fall on top of him when the jack skidded. A nurse is leaning over him and tries over and over again to see whether he has any reflexes. She calls, 'Open your eyes, open your eyes,' in her strong country accent, but he does nothing.

The days and weeks after the accident can be described from various points of view : physical and psychological; then publicity and Ferrari.

Physical : between the time when I was dragged out of the flames and arrival at the Intensive Care Unit many mistakes were made. But after that everything was the best possible : marvellous doctors, marvellous nursing, a strong will-to-live on my side – and luck of course. With scorched lungs it's a question of life and death, and if it's 'life' recovery is relatively quick. The burns were more of a cosmetic problem. The most important skin grafts from the upper thigh to the face were made as soon as I was out of danger, and were very successful. I couldn't stick the hospital another minute. I got heavy doses of valium but only slept two hours. The understanding of the doctors about it was grand; they believed me when I said I could only recover at home. I was smuggled secretly out of the hospital clinic and flown to Salzburg. People who telephoned were put off; for days only a handful of people knew that I was already at home. I slept for six hours right away – home is incomparable. I have no illusions about myself, hobbling with a stick and having pain where the skin was removed, and I am not very handsome, because my right thigh is on my face. But that doesn't worry me.

After that the rhythm of recovery was much faster. It only took six weeks to get well, largely because of Willy Dungl and his therapy, also because I was so impatient to get back into normal life that I cooperated as much as I could, in Salzburg and on Ibiza where the sea helped too. Psychologically, the fact that I was alive was so much more wonderful than horror at my appearance, that my burns were never a problem of that sort. I judged by my bodily recovery, not my appearance, whether to start seeing people again. If they were shocked, that was their problem. Every handicapped person has a right to exercise his profession, and society should help him, not hinder him. In any case I decided that the 'cosmetic' side of the accident was of secondary importance.

Family: Marlene's presence in the hospital helped me tremendously – it gave me a lift. Those days also brought me closer to my parents and my brother.

Publicity: the effect on the fans was colossal, 99% helpful, encouraging, often touching. People wrote and telephoned offering their skin, or their ears, told me their experiences of burns and skin transplants. A little boy sent me his toy Ferrari, because he had heard mine was burnt.

As for the journalists, there were wide differences between them. The hyenas among them behaved in a way that went beyond everything. They tried all ways to get a photograph of my unrecognizable swollen head. The hospital was besieged, they had to creep in unnoticed, they tried to bribe the nurses.

Bild went on for weeks with its special Lauda accident reports. Headlines were : 'Niki Lauda's fight with death, "My God, where is my face?" ' And in the text 'Niki Lauda, the fastest racing driver in the world, hasn't got a face now – it is nothing but raw flesh, the eyes are popping out.' This was illustrated with two nice photographs of my face covered in bandages, naturally on the front page. Two days later *Bild* readers were given good news with the headlines 'Niki Lauda will pull through . . . but how can a man live without a face?' In the text it went on :

'How can he go on living with no face? However frightful it may sound, even when his body has recovered, he won't be able to see anyone for six months. Only by 1979 will his new face be ready. Nose, eyelids, lips will be made, but this face will not resemble his former face. Only by his voice will his friends be able to recognise the racing driver.'

Ferrari : The reaction was partly moving and human, partly chaotic, partly vile. Daniele Audetto, who knew nothing about it, gave a statement about security in which he said the accident had resulted from a driving mistake. Then the wreck was so complete that nothing could be discovered from that. Even when amateurs' ciné-films were developed they didn't give the answer hundred per cent sure, though they point to the likelihood of a defect in the car. As far as I go, I say I don't know, I remember nothing. Audetto ought to have spoken the truth, which is that nobody will ever know exactly what happened.

One important aspect has been either wrongly described or not described at all. The English in particular were critical and said the Ferrari had caught fire, that the petrol tank had broken away and so forth. Maybe there are cars with better fire protection than Ferrari, but I believe that any racing car which crashes into a bank at 200 km an hour must reckon with the fact that its tank is unlikely to survive unburnt. What seems to me much more important is that I broke no bones, and that I am alive. The robust, strong construction of the Ferrari saved my life. I can't think of any other Formula I car in 1976 whose driver could have survived such crashes and collisions.

In this case the steel frame which reinforces the aluminium saved the day. The luxury of so much strength (which has the disadvantage of added weight) had at that time only been achieved by Ferrari – and that I am here to thank them for it is the huge and well-earned success of the Ferrari designers.

As far as the behaviour of the Ferrari team during my hospital time goes, it wavered between assurances 'your car will always be yours' and lightning negotiations with Fittipaldi and Peterson to replace me. Because of their fury over a decision of the sport authorities (recognizing Hunt's victory at Jarama) and also because of muddle and perplexity Ferrari announced that it was abandoning Formula I racing. This helped nobody, and me least of all. Then it was obvious that they would only be represented at one or two Grands Prix, and that Austria wasn't among them. At the peak of this chaotic time Audetto telephoned several Austrian journalists that they ought to get the race at Zeltweg cancelled, and prevent other drivers getting world championship points while Niki Lauda was out of action.

10. Coup de Grâce?

There was only one thing to be done, to concentrate a hundred per cent on recovery, in Salzburg, on Ibiza, always with Willy Dungl, always obeying the doctors, all this was the task of those weeks. What else could I have done? Lie in bed and look in the mirror?

My first press conference was horrible. 'What did your wife say when she saw your face?' asked one of them. You could get up and go or else give stupid answers. Had Marlene asked for a divorce, had I got complexes about my appearance, what was going to happen about my ear – even the most primitive tact or good manners were apparently forgotten when talking of Lauda. I find it obvious that one should treat a cripple in a normal manner and not keep referring to his imperfection. People are sometimes surprised that I am so 'cold' or 'hard', but you have to be damned hard to deal with these sort of situations. I answered the question 'how I was going to get used to my face' by saying I didn't need a face, only a right foot. What other answer could one give to such an idiot? And nobody seems to realize that the answer follows from the question, they all think I am a hard devil.

I had decided that if it was only a question of my looks, I wasn't going to let that stop my normal life.

Thirty-eight days after the accident I reported to Ferrari. A little melodrama on my arrival, and with the waiting fans, but above all, perplexity. None of them, from the Commendatore down, knew what to do with me. I didn't fit into their scheme of things. Was I abnormally ambitious? Was I insensitive, frightening people with my appearance? Did I harm our profession, because the accident showed on my face? And above all, what sort of Lauda was I now? A new one, naturally. Had I become cowardly? Would I crack up? Was I full of complexes and therefore unpredictable? How must they regard me? Should they look at my burns openly or secretly? Was I somebody who'd been shot and instead of lying there rushes forward to be finished off?

Only the simplest answer seemed impossible for them to grasp : I felt I was fit, the doctors agreed, and therefore I wanted to get back to work as quickly as possible.

Ferrari's perplexity was all the greater because they had already made Carlos Reutemann Lauda's substitute, and it was very awkward if I upset their plans. With Lauda you couldn't be sure of anything, and how could you suddenly have a three-driver-team?

Those days for me were a key experience at Ferrari's; nothing was frank and above board, but underhand, as in water polo. The Old Man never said openly to my face that he didn't want me to drive at Monza, yet afterwards he counted it my biggest mistake. Without my early 'comeback' we could have lost the world championship with style, we should have been so to speak the moral winners, since the man lying in bed was helpless. I lost this chance by coming back so soon. Such are the complicated ways their minds work at Ferrari's, always worried about what people will say, or what will be in the newspapers. Opinion about a thing became more important for them than the thing itself, so the way was full of twists and turns because nobody was sure where it was going.

Not only Ferrari was put out by my decision, six weeks

after Nürburgring, to drive at Monza. Serious journalists, usually on my side, overwhelmed me with questions. An example from the Vienna *Presse* :

Crazy?

What to do about his left ear he doesn't yet know; He confided to a Vienna journalist 'it won't go into the helmet because of the scars. New skin hasn't grown there and it hurts like hell.' Perhaps the specially ordered new helmet will have a sort of built-in head-phone?

Niki Lauda is worried. His skull is bald, the curly hair shaved off. For once, it wasn't aerodynamics that reached for the scissors. Lauda's hair went west on 1st August in the 'green hell' called Nürburgring. For days the doctors fought to keep Nikolaus Lauda, born 22/2/49, alive. The head burns of the dare-devil racing driver were severe. Skin grafts were necessary, and it's still going on. He won't show himself in public yet. He hides from the curious. As well as his prominent teeth there are burn marks and stitches, no eyebrows, and a blood-encrusted ear. One understands that he keeps aloof for the moment, and one shares his suffering.

With his therapist Lauda journeys to a Mediterranean island in the sun, a prescription which has cured rheumatics. Early next week, however, this brave man will sit once again in his 'flying coffin' and start practice at Fiorano. Because his goal is Monza, where Lauda hopes once again to challenge fate. Still disfigured, perhaps for always with his blood-encrusted ear, but with a 'normal blood count' as he expresses it.

To the question whether Lauda's ordeal by fire in the Eifel injured not only his head but also his brain Lauda's answer is that he is on top of things as never before. Crazy !

Getting back into the racing car : I had to improvise the helmet, my burnt ear was frightfully tender, I had to pack it round with foam rubber cushions. Everyone stood around staring in an embarrassed way while I climbed into the car, and was strapped in, and drove away. No special feeling. The car was an old gherkin with a bad engine and the track was dirty. I drove forty laps, and noticed nothing different, nothing new or abnormal. But these few laps at Fiorano didn't mean much. On the home track it is only 'abstract' driving, the serious fight is missing. As finger exercises however these laps were okay.

Friday practice at Monza : so much rain and water on the track that everything was irregular. I was afraid and found an excuse to go into the pits. But that was nothing, because the conditions were grotesque.

To make things a bit more complicated and depressing, the organizers insisted that I must be passed by the doctors. I had to go to Milan; an eye specialist, a specialist in circulation, and a psychiatrist all had to examine me. The conclusion of these learned men : I am fit. Saturday practice : the real threshold, the real test. Now came the usual 'pressure' of such days, in addition to the 'threshold', that is easy to say. When a Formula I goes really fast, 'feeling' doesn't mean much. When a Formula I car skids, you can either master it or you can't. The first time the Ferrari skidded I was scared. That is a frightful way to react, and I thought of a pilot who had survived an accident and who was back in his airplane for the first time and is scared of an air pocket. Being scared was intolerable. I said to myself : you can't drive a car like that. Then I waited quite consciously for the skid and began with the precision work of the drift. After that it was not so hard, the worst was behind me. I had crossed the threshold and was once more at my normal *niveau*.

Next day I was fourth in the race, which some people thought was quite good.

11. Interim

Restless days. I still had pain with my burnt ear, and with my wrist; as a result of the skin graft I had trouble with my right eye. Nothing serious, but I couldn't quite shut it when I slept, because the new skin 'drew' the eyelid; therefore there was the danger of the pupil drying up.

There were also good results. One handicap, left over from my tractor accident, was cured. In the mornings after I got up I could never move my left hand. This was something to do with a nerve connected to my backbone; anyway this rather comic handicap quite worried me. After the Nürburgring accident it was blown away. People talk of 'Heat cures'!

I took my flying pilot's test and was pleased when I got through. Not very important perhaps, and some might ask whether I hadn't got more than that to worry about. I had put off the test again and again during the past two years, simply for lack of time to collect the obligatory thirty hours practice. It had been the same this year, and I didn't want to waste the flying hours once again. I had flown all over Europe in a twin-engined machine (with a pilot sitting beside me) and never bought a ticket. So I was relieved when everything was cleared up and I passed the test successfully.

At Ferrari's Clay Regazzoni got his notice to quit, the new man for 1977 was Reutemann. I was sorry to see Regazzoni go, we were on very good terms; we weren't exactly friends but we never got annoyed with each other.

I did my best for Clay with the Old Man, but I had no chance, they were all angry and unforgiving. I think at the end the last straw was a series of interviews Regazzoni gave. A couple of times he made his opinion of the sport leadership at Ferrari's pretty clear, and that is suicide in this team, where newspaper reading is so important. His notice to quit was of course done up with red roses; they didn't want to stand in his way for free decisions for next year, and so forth; 'he is free' and such like touching statements. Even the smooth ending of a contract leads to a theatrical show which is super-imposed on reality in such a way that outsiders can't judge, and even the actors can't either. Ten years before John Surtees, World Champion for the year 1964 in a Ferrari, was sacked at the end of the season. For many reasons, among them that he had criticized Ferrari too freely to the press. Ferrari's press man, Ghozzi, had the job of handing Surtees his dismissal after the Belgian Grand Prix. But it so happened that John won the race, and Ghozzi simply couldn't bring himself to give him the sack, and went home. The next opportunity was at Le Mans. In the middle of practice Dragoni, the team manager, told Surtees he must get out of his car and let Scarfiotti, that is to say a man in the second class, drive. Surtees was furious and wanted to know what was up. We'll have a talk after practice, said Dragoni. Surtees was still furious and said he wouldn't put up with such a thing. 'Thank you very much,' said Dragoni 'there's the door.' Surtees was fired.

Back to Autumn 1976.

Clay was not to be stopped and he still drove, under his contract, in the overseas races. Then the Ferrari troubles came to a peak. Because of my accident we had an annoying lag in testing, there was no sign of the former Ferrari superiority any more. Then we had suspension problems in Canada, and in any case I came home with only four points (a third place at Watkins Glen). We had a demoralized team, perplexed by James Hunt's superiority. James had won both races, he was only three points behind me. The decisive race was the last, in Fuji (Japan) and this upset my plans. I should have liked the season to end sooner. However we all pulled ourselves together once more, tested a lot in Italy, got a modified front wheel suspension and were full of 'fighting spirit' as we flew over to Japan.

12. Fuji

Rain, rain rain. The first warming-up practice only to try it out. I go straight into the pits, because it's madness to drive here. All but three drivers are against starting. Talk, discussion, quarrels, up and down and to and fro. Organizers, team leaders, drivers. Second warming-up practice, only a few go out, I don't.

It is pure craziness to drive in so much water; you lose all sense of direction because you can't see, and you get aquaplaning, the car swivels round and you don't know why. You can no longer direct the car with your hands or with your head, because you get into situations where there's nothing to be done. You try to drive straight and you suddenly swerve left, right, backwards, you can't be sure in which direction.

Hectic arguments and quarrels to and fro, television, you must remember television. Once they say: 'It's after two, and at five it will be dark, so we must start now.' Madness. They debate for five hours, consider this and consider that, and suddenly all these ideas go by the board because it's half past two. Start in five minutes, they say. It was raining less now, and apparently the whole track has had the water brushed away, but that was an attempt which basically changed nothing.

Warming-up lap before the start, we drive quite slowly. Near me Watson suddenly takes off and lands in the field : aquaplaning. Streams run over the track, and on these streams you are as helpless as a paper boat and you begin again as best you can. One thought makes me go : perhaps we shall soon get a dry bit, that would help. But at the start it rains harder than ever.

You can hardly hold the car. You can see that there's a stream across the track, you can go to the right and drive by the rails, through the water, all this at 150, and then when you've shipped a lot of water you get caught sooner or later, perhaps on the track, perhaps in the field, perhaps on the guard rails.

I drive slowly, keep away from the other cars so that none of them shall run into me, think how stupid this race is. I am not going to drive at this pace any longer, even going slowly you could be washed away. After the second lap I go into the pits. Forghieri leans down and asks me what's up. I am not going to drive, I say, because it's madness, it's just not on.

He quickly suggests, 'We'll pretend you've got engine trouble.'

'No,' say I, 'if I don't drive I shall say I don't want to drive, I don't need excuses.'

I am convinced Forghieri wished me well when he suggested we give engine trouble as the reason for not going on, he wasn't setting a trap for me. But in the end it would have been disastrous for me if I had done what he suggested. At least when I gave my notice, and again thousands of times, the story would have been thrown at me, 'We protected him, the coward, and that's the thanks we get.'

I stand in the pits and look out. After a while the rain stops. I don't blame myself, it was the right decision. It could easily have been fatal in the first laps, with dead and injured and the race abandoned. This danger was so obvious that it is immaterial whether these accidents happened or not. The possibility of catastrophe was simply too great. The rain stopping – unforeseeable – was my personal bad luck; I consider I had bad luck, not that I made a mistake.

We have to go off early to catch our airplane. Marlene, Forghieri and I are in the car. If Hunt is fifth or worse, I am still World Champion. When we drove away Hunt was in the lead, but with tyre change nothing is yet settled. From the car radio we gather that Hunt has fallen behind. After that, nothing more about the Grand Prix. A quarter of an hour later the race result is announced and at that very moment our car goes into the underpass near the airport and we can't hear.

Only at the airport the Ferrari man gives the news : Hunt is World Champion. I'd had bad luck. At the moment I hardly minded. I can't begin to cry because the rain happened to stop.

Forghieri and I rang up the Old Man from Tokyo airport. I told him my feelings, my reasons, I told him it would have been madness to go on. He was very realistic, said aha, yes, yes, hm, yes yes, goodbye; he said not a word against me or against my decision, but he also gave not a grain of comfort or the slightest help. He never said, 'Don't worry.' And it would have been marvellous if he had.

I could just about guess what it was like when Ferrari laid down the receiver. The usual storm.

I only got the tip of it; officially the Old Man stood firm behind my decision, but that didn't help me really. After all those days and weeks of recovery after the accident my firm was blowing hot and cold, though it was all wrapped up in pretence and the show was not the reality.

Naturally in their heart of hearts they didn't agree with

my decision. Even good friends like Luca Montezemolo thought Lauda is finished, he can't do it any more, he's too cowardly, he's had too much of a shock. My decision didn't fit the notion : win races or give up racing. Not to drive, to think it over and give up, that was too much for them.

The Ferrari underground simmered.

I couldn't worry about it too much because the operation on my right eye couldn't be put off any longer. While I was still in the St Gallen clinic, Luca Montezemolo told me from which direction the danger threatened : They want to make you team manager. And Luca − so serious was the situation − was even himself a little bit sold on this plan, he was wavering. The idea was adventurous, because it would solve all Ferrari's worries at my expense. They were afraid I wasn't as good as I had been, and therefore they preferred to get another driver, but they were also afraid of the opposite, and that in another team I should be a dangerous opponent. As team manager I could perhaps be used for testing, they would have me under their control, and I would not be dangerous.

It was the worst time. The pressure from Japan was still upon me, I was worried about my eye, I didn't know what the result of the operation would be. And on top of everything, this hit below the belt. I said to Luca : 'If you don't want me to drive for you, let me free at once from my contract, and I'll leave immediately. There's no question of me being team manager.'

Luca no longer wavered; he was once more on my side, told the 'underground' my answer − and with this the case was settled. Not, though, the attitude of Ferrari towards me.

Hardly were my eye bandages off, hardly could I see again, than I flew to Bologna, to present myself and to discuss the future. It was obvious that we should have to test, test, and test again, if we were going to catch up with the arrears of our car. I was up and about, the world championship was

(continued on page 79)

Comments on the following picture series

63 The first somersault (spring 1969 in Vienna—Aspern): "I was crazy, was horny and lusting for driving, wanted to pass where you should not pass. . . ." Notice the plain jumpsuit reflecting Lauda's market value in the second year of his career: zero.

64 Charming Vienna boy from a good family: 1969.

65 Formula 2 season at March (1971).

66 For seven years at Niki's side: Mariella Reininghaus.

67 1973: Under Louis Stanley in the BRM team.

68 Lauda's master mechanic for four years at Ferrari, Ermanno Cuoghi.

69 1975: With Enzo Ferrari (above); Mauro Forghieri (below left) and Luca Montezemolo (middle).

70 Marlene's first appearance at the track in the beginning of 1976.

71 For Lauda the twin engine Cessna Golden Eagle (below) was only an interim solution before he had the Citation (above).

72 August 1, 1976, kilometer 10.6 on the Nürburgring: All of a sudden the Ferrari branched off to the right, penetrated the guard rail, crashed against the slope, bounced again over the entire track and caught fire.

73 Rescue by a race course guard, Guy Edwards, Brett Lunger and Arturo Merzario "who walks through the flames like the good Lord and succeeds in opening my safety-belt. . . ."

74 Emphasis on privacy: the Lauda house in Hof near Salzburg.

75-77 Chez Niki.

78 The gas station of Bauer-Gustl with Lauda's trophies; the Bentley is only there for polishing, preserving and joking; motorbike riding as a recreational sport.

63

71

Privat!

Privatweg
Durchgang
verboten!

Vorsicht
bissiger
Hund!

(continued from page 61)

over and done with as far as I went; for me what counted was the coming season and getting ready for it.

When I asked for the programme, I got the answer that Reutemann was to test during the coming week at Paul Ricard. Fine, I said, I'll be there. Then they drew back and twisted and turned and finally said unfortunately there's only one car. Carlos should drive on the first and second days, I on the third day. Nothing was said against this.

I had another press conference about my show, and I told among other things that we were off again, and about Paul Ricard and so on. When I got back to Salzburg there was a telegram in the office from Ferrari, with more or less this text : 'We learn from the newspapers that you are planning to test at Paul Ricard. This does not conform with our test programme. You must be that day at Fiorano.' There was not even a personal signature, only 'race section'.

It couldn't have been made more obvious to a driver that he had been pushed down to second place, and must knuckle under. Impossible to treat someone who has just got over an operation and is ready to begin again, in a more brutal way. I was crazy : it couldn't be true. While the great Reutemann did great work at Ricard, I was to go round and round Fiorano.

I telephoned Enzo Ferrari and had the most decisive talk that I had in all my four years with Ferrari. What did this mean? I asked. Well, he said, since I (Lauda) had made a wrong decision, all decisions henceforward were to come from him, he would take it in hand himself. Wrong decision, what did he mean? Monza, he said; I shouldn't have raced at Monza. If I had missed the race because of my accident we should have lost the world championship in a way that would have looked better. I was utterly furious and shouted at him that perhaps for an Italian it would be all right to lie in bed and in bed to lose in a way that looked well, but when I fight

I fight, and I don't lie in bed. If I lose the world championship on the road, well I accept it. Thanks, goodbye, I slammed the receiver down.

A little later Ghedini rang up, full of complaints, the Old Man is raging, everything is finished, he's chucking you out. Telephone at once and apologize. No question of that, I say, I'm not going to apologize.

I was all in, depressed and furious. Why had I been through hell, got myself out of hospital, worked every minute on my body to recover, given everything I had to it, just to be treated in this way at the end of it all. Naturally when the Old Man said Monza he meant Fuji. If at Fuji I had driven like an angel through the water, everything would have been grand. I tried to put myself in his shoes. Okay, he pays for Ferrari to race and Ferrari to win. He pays for the world championship, and then all of a sudden the fool won't drive because it's too dangerous for him. But when I go on thinking as Ferrari must be thinking, I can't help coming to the human situation, for after all he's got a man under contract, not an ape. He can give the ape a kick up the arse and order him to drive, but a man must be expected to think. And if he didn't consider me an idiot before, then he must accept the result of my thoughts. When I think over the whole picture, including the Nürburgring, and when I add the quite special pressures on Niki Lauda in that autumn of 1976 and look back on it all, I can't see one iota of a possibility of it being fair to punish me for Fuji.

His decisions are not even the right ones if you set aside everything human and simply judge by professional criteria in the hardest possible way. Even then, we lost the world championship together; not only in Fuji, but also in France, where his crankshaft broke, and in Monza, where my teammate Regazzoni wouldn't let me pass.

In those days my fury against Ferrari was so deep that from

then on I never again felt happy in the team. Too much was broken. I was of the opinion that I had done more than just what was necessary for Ferrari. I had given everything that was in me to our work. I had always tried to keep out of the underground intrigues, out of all the Ferrari politics. I was extremely careful not to say a single word against Ferrari in public, and I stuck to that, unlike all the other drivers – and despite the fact that there were a damned lot of reasons for me to complain of Ferrari.

There was also the breach of trust in November 1976. It didn't help much when a telegram came to say the programme was changed and I was expected at Paul Ricard. He had withdrawn, he was afraid. Naturally I flew there. Then it rained and I never was able to test, but I had established the principle. I hadn't allowed myself as 'finished' and as number two to be coolly shot down.

There were also troubles on other fronts. I met the chief of the mineral water firm Römerquelle to sign the sponsor and advertisement agreement for next year. I had been a good partner, when I won in Monaco I drank Römerquelle and not champagne in front of the television cameras, and tried to give value for money. Now the man said : I shall pay you less for 1977, because you will only drive at the back. I thought quickly and came to the conclusion that it was already too late to get another main sponsor for 1977, so I signed. I also signed an agreement to pay a penalty if I wore any other cap except Römerquelle cap, except on the podium after a victory, because then we had to wear Goodyear caps, as long as Goodyear provided us with tyres.

This was one more example of the way they all try to crucify you the moment your position is slightly weaker. This business of the cap was a bombshell. My forehead, my skin and my ears looked so awful that he was certain sure I should never show myself without a cap – he would therefore get super advertising. On television, under the strong lights in the studio, I was sometimes so hot that I took the cap off; which in the beginning rather horrified people. But then my hair grew again, and the skin on my forehead got a bit better, and people got used to it.

One year later, when I was once more on top, I didn't sign again for Römerquelle.

*

Praise for the World Champion, James Hunt. He is of all the drivers the one I like best. I value him, I am fond of him, he is the only one I know fairly well in private life. He is relaxed, easy and unworried. He does what amuses him, and I like that. All the quarrels between McLaren and Ferrari in 1976 never made any difference to James and me personally. We had divergent interests and each had to fight for his own side, of course, but that had nothing to do with us two men. He is a marvellous driver and brilliantly talented. When he is rested, he is the hardest man to beat.

13. The New Man

Audetto, because of his muddles, occasional blackouts and bossiness, had become unbearable as team manager. Even for the Commendatore, who already, after the Fuji flop might have fired him; there wasn't much difference of opinion here. Audetto wasn't unemployed; a job at Fiat as sport director and chief of the rally teams awaited him.

The post of Ferrari team manager was nominally shared between Sante Ghedini, a very reliable and practical man, and a new man, Roberto Nosetto. Nosetto got the job because he had worked at Ferrari's for twenty years; Ferrari is so to speak his life's complex. He said he only had one goal and that was to work for Ferrari, Ferrari was his all in all. He is a man who would willingly *die* for Ferrari, and that's a mistake, because one shouldn't die for Ferrari, one should struggle with Ferrari so that something intelligent happens. Nosetto I found even more annoying than Audetto, because of his obsession with the colour green. He is so superstitious that he only wears green things, if possible from his cap to his shoes, though he has to wear the team uniform (with yellow Ferrari anorak). Whenever I looked at him I saw green. As team manager he was a joke figure. His superstition passed all bounds. Before the Swedish Grand Prix the team was in the depths; we were bad as never before. Reutemann started from twelfth place and I from fifteenth. I should imagine this must have been the all-time low in the entire history of the firm of Ferrari, a firm unaccustomed to failure. We were outsiders, our cars were hopeless. Before the start, when I was already in the car, Nosetto bent over me and wanted to shove a bit of green stuff in the cockpit: 'To bring you luck, you'll win with this,' he said. I shouted, 'It's lucky for you that I'm strapped in, otherwise I'd hit you.'

Nosetto's superstition forbids him to drive in any car which has anything to do with the number seven. Whenever he hires a car, if there is a seven on its number-plate he tries to change to another. If that isn't possible he sticks something over the seven.

You couldn't argue with him, and towards the end of the season he simply ceased to exist as far as I went, he was nothing but a speck of green.

Psychologically therefore the atmosphere in the team was no better than before. Reutemann wasn't much help there, from the first day we had nothing to say to each other. We had only the absolutely necessary contact.

The beginning was especially hard. Reutemann was favourite; they thought that at the Grand Prix in Argentina and Brazil he would drive me to a standstill. Before the journey to Argentina Forghieri gave me the tip to watch the way Reutemann drove, observe him in practice, at Buenos Aires he is unbeatable. I had the role of the half blind or the semi-idiot. Apart from this psychological pressure I found the situation rather exciting. It was a real *challenge*.

Unfortunately the chances of learning a lot from Reutemann at Buenos Aires were rather more limited than Forghieri had imagined. From the very beginning I was faster in practice than Carlos. When Reutemann knocked down six catch fence posts and bent his Ferrari, the Ferrari world-picture was changed. In the race itself both of our cars played the expected inferior role. I withdrew after twenty laps with a fault in the fuel injection; Carlos fought his way through the field of more or less damaged cars and arrived third behind Scheckter and Pace.

When we got home, I saw in the eyes of my Italian friends doubts about the practice times; they couldn't quite believe that Reutemann hadn't got me under. Oh well, first race of the season, and so forth. Naturally, I said, it's going to happen.

Then came Brazil – Reutemann's great firework. After a few average laps during the first practice they gave him a new rear wing, which straight away made the car more driveable. He started from the front row of the grid, defeated James Hunt and was a radiant victor. The first Ferrari triumph for many months, immense enthusiasm! I was in the dog house : thirteenth in practice (my worst ever with Ferrari) a third place in the race, without the slightest chance of getting within striking distance of the leaders.

The psychological pressure of having been written off didn't prevent me from thinking, and analysing the situation. And this analysis, in short, was : Thirteenth practice place (compared with Reutemann's second) sounds depressing, but it has reasons which can be explained. First the handling problem, which Carlos also had, then on the Saturday, the fuel pipe broke and I sat in the middle of the muck. I got out of the petrol-soaked car into a reserve car, which was even worse, hopeless. And there was only one of these new rear wings. Carlos only made his tremendous leap forward the moment it was fitted on his car. Worse than the visible depth of starting thirteenth seemed to me, the entire level of development of our cars. It is not a solution, when at the last moment Forghieri produces a rear wing out of his hat. It was obvious that the cars had other problems. The solution we thought we saw lay in the aerodynamics, not in the suspension or the tyres. Nevertheless everything was so unclear, so muddled and dependent on chance, that I considered our position was quite bad. Despite the fact that Reutemann was leading in the world championship.

I had a serious discussion with the Old Man, and I impressed upon him that for the next race, South Africa, everything must be properly tested on the spot, and by me. 'If nothing is done on the development side we shall never win another race.' Enzo Ferrari believed me at that moment, and he agreed to the detailed tests at Kyalami. With Lauda.

It was one of my best races, my greatest victory.

14. Kyalami

I awake with the marvellous feeling that I am going to win. A nice day. I know too why everything seems so good, it's because I haven't got a worse car than the others, so that I can drive among those in front. Practice has made this obvious. I am in the second row and nobody but me knows that I am 'underrated' and that this car really belongs in the front row. During practice I did slightly less well than I should have, for various reasons, among them too much traffic during the decisive laps and so forth. In such circumstances it is nice to be in the second row, you've got a wonderful secret.

The rush of the start. When they are all sorted out, I am second; good. Good for the moment and good for the whole day. Hunt in front, Scheckter behind; rather too big in my driving mirror but not yet threatening. One must be careful. At the S bend Hunt is uncannily quick, he draws away from me, second time round definitely so. But just there I won't let him get away, because soon after comes the straight, the best chance for overtaking, and I must be right behind him there. If he makes a small mistake that's no use to me if I am two lengths behind, I can't take advantage of the situation. In order to be prepared for any eventuality I must sit on his tail, therefore I must do the S as fast as he does; the rest of the track is no problem. I concentrate on the S and force myself to drive as fast as he does. Now I am right on his neck. In the seventh lap he touches the edge and makes a little jerk, and I know this will slow him up slightly, now's my chance, I stay a moment in his windstream and then I've got him. I am leading, out in front, the first time for ages, ever since my accident.

Now, look out, stay calm. I must use the situation. Get up steam and go. I drive a few laps flat out, until I'm four and a half seconds in front of Hunt. I see a new sign in the Ferrari pits: Scheckter is second. Disagreeable, because it's a new challenge. It could mean that Scheckter had been held up hitherto by something or other, and that he's really faster than Hunt. Perhaps he will press harder than Hunt. Yes, I get more pressure, Jody is only two seconds behind now. On the straight there's a little hump. Just as I go over it, I see something lying on the track, it looks hard and metallic. It could be a little snake, but then I feel the bump: I have touched the thing. Otherwise nothing is to be seen at the moment. I make the belt a bit looser so that I can sit higher and see the nose better. I can see the front wing now but no change. I make the belt fast. I don't understand what's happening. I see debris on the track, but only a few hundred metres further on two cars at the side. I think: Pryce and Laffite have had a crash. But the debris, why was that there?

At the next bend the Ferrari tried like mad to go straight on. The wing must be damaged I thought that's why it's understeering so badly. That I'd hit something was obvious. But how serious was it? Or is the wishbone perhaps damaged? I drive a bit slower. During this time Scheckter has closed up and now he looms large in my mirror. It's all over, I thought. But at the moment there's no change. Perhaps I should try again to discover what has happened; I try with all my concentration but it doesn't help, the car is handling badly, the understeer is awful. Pits? At many other races I should have gone into the pits now, to have a look, to get repaired.

But my accident had made me tougher, I've got more in reserve for such occasions.

I decide not to go into the pits, not to give in, not to relax. First to try and keep my lead over Scheckter. The problem is the understeer. Where could he overtake me? Only with a rush on the straight, where I passed James. Nowhere else on the circuit would it be possible. Therefore I must concentrate on the corner before the straight. I go slower into the bend. He can sit as close behind me as he likes, it won't help him, because if I go slower the car doesn't handle so badly so I can put the power on earlier and enter the straight under full acceleration. Slower, slower still into the bend, on no account slide, and now FLAT OUT on the accelerator, a rush forward, a glance in the mirror: yes, he's two lengths behind.

On each lap the situation is just as critical; I mustn't go into the bends too fast. Otherwise the understeer is so bad that I have to lift off, and then there's no gap under acceleration, and that's what Jody is waiting for, just as I waited for it with Hunt. I mustn't slide. The system worked quite well, so well that I am gaining a tenth of a second on each lap. I have got into the way of this comic car. After a while, I have pulled out three seconds on Scheckter.

The red light when I brake at the end of the straight. It can't be true. I have a better look but can see nothing more. Next lap when I put the brakes on: red light again, and no oil pressure. Shit. How many laps to go? Twenty-six. All over, forget it, you can forget the race, you've no hope now. Then I think: Oh well, go on as long as you can. It's difficult, and tiring, always to be winding yourself up for nothing, to give all you've got when you know it has no sense. All the same, let's see how we go. What can I do about the oil pressure? First I brake fifty metres before the end of a straight. Quite good. The oil pressure doesn't fall, but the red light goes on. I have to compensate for braking sooner by taking the corner faster. Jody isn't catching up, so I go into the curve with everything I've got. At some of the corners I take out the clutch. Then accelerate, as soon as possible.

The little red light gets worse. It goes on the whole time, not only on left hand bends but on right hand bends as well; I've hardly any proper oil pressure.

How many more laps? Ten. No chance, madness, this can't last. Please, please stop now, at once – don't do it to me, don't pack up and stop just half a lap before the finish. Stop now, you brute. But the car goes on. I don't look down any more, otherwise it's just too awful when I see the red light. The same with the tachometer; I was only pulling ten thousand revolutions, I could feel it without any indicator, and I spared myself the sight of the dreadful red light. I could only think of swear words. Stop now or not at all you pig. Only four more laps, that gives a spark of hope. Three laps, two laps, perhaps I'll make it. The last lap, please, you've only got to get into the straight and accelerate in third gear, that must do the trick, because I could take it out of gear and roll to the finish, that would be possible. I see red on the dashboard, but the car is still going, through the succession of corners at the back of the circuit, right, then left, into the S, accelerate just once more out of the slow right hander at ten thousand I put it into third, take it straight out and roll on to the finish. The first victory since my accident!

I brake at once, no joy, no lap of honour. I jump out and look under the car to see what's the matter. In old days I shouldn't have done that. I should have whispered into the mechanic Tomaini's ear : 'Something's gone wrong, there's something under the car.' But in the last few months I am no longer so sensitive. I don't care whether people watching television see there's something wrong with the car. Yes, the roll over bar off Tom Pryce's car has been driven into the radiator. Later I heard from the mechanics what had happened : instead of 14 litres of water there were only three, instead of eight litres of oil, only one and a half. Normally the car would just stop, in such conditions.

At the prize-giving Goodyear's man Baldwin told me Tom Pryce is dead. A crazy accident; because of a marshal, who ran across the track. The misery over his death and the joy over my victory mingled to something indescribable.

Ecclestone had organized a helicopter. I fly straight to the airport, where Swissair is just starting. In Zürich my own jet is waiting. At home, a telegram from the Old Man : 'You are still yourself – as before, but more than ever !'

Such rubbish. He sent the telegram not for me but only because his car had come in first. He didn't congratulate me on my work, but on the lucky chance that the thing hadn't packed up. If the machine had bust at the last corner my achievement would have been exactly the same. But there would have been no telegram.

I didn't give a damn for such telegrams, they say nothing to me. And they don't express the man's real feelings. He should send me a telegram each time, that would be different. To comfort me when I've lost, that would be better.

15. Pressure

Long Beach: In a chaotic lap I push the car round the circuit in 1.21,63 minutes, and this time was five hundredths of a second faster than Andretti. To think it over is senseless, none of us can imagine what five hundredths of a second means. All the same I rather like the dimension of unreality, what cannot be grasped in this sort of driving, to shake it all off and plunge into the chaotic world with its jammed wheels, late braking, changed borders and rasping of the stone kerbs. For the achievement which you can hardly express, you get the equivalent in a dimension you can't grasp: five hundredths of a second, hearty congratulations Herr Lauda, you are quickest in practice, a hundred bottles of champagne and pole position.

There was nothing one could say against the car at Long Beach, it suited the day, the weather and the circuit. First time since the accident that I'm first in practice! On the day of the race I felt tremendous pressure, actually inexplicable. Perhaps it was my pole position, which carries with it a sort of *responsibility*: the responsibilty of making the best start, of leading and of winning.

I made a hash of the start. I was so far forward that I had to look right up above me in order to be able to see the starting light. Those behind me could see the lamp as well as their tachometers. I could only look up or down, and when I looked up and saw the green light, my revolutions were right low down. Long Beach is like Monaco as far as overtaking goes. Without goodwill from the man in front you have hardly a hope of getting by. I made another mistake in this race, and perhaps pressure was to blame. You could translate pressure as being in bad form, but I don't feel in bad form whereas I do feel 'pressure', and in my opinion it is a noticeable frame of mind which presses upon me. Anyway it wasn't my day; when I wanted to make good the bad start, and out-brake Andretti, I braked too hard, the car over-braked in front and the front wheels jammed, and the tyre is no longer hundred per cent round, so that you get vibrations right through the whole car, and especially the steering wheel, you've got a pneumatic air drill, not a steering wheel.

I was second, behind Andretti, and in Italy had to listen to them saying I had made a mess of the race. This time it was true, I might have driven better, I could have won if I'd made no mistakes.

Jarama, practice for the Spanish Grand Prix; a left hand corner, ugh, a blow in the small of the back, a devilish pain, a cracking sound. I make it as far as the pits, can hardly breathe. Grajales! The doctor must come. A helicopter takes me to hospital.*

The pain was so diabolical that even when I was vomiting I speculated on what this mysterious injury could be. Apart

* At the Nürburgring accident the 6th and 7th ribs were broken. Because of the lung damage and burns the ribs healed while I was lying down, which is not ideal. If they heal when you are lying down some of the natural elasticity and articulation of the ribs is lost. At Jarama, almost a year later, various things happened at the same moment: strong centrifugal force held me in position, and when owing to an uneven surface I got a knock, there was not the slightest spring or give in my body. At the same time the interaction of the braced muscles caused terrific pain − nerve pain which led to non-functioning of the muscles between the ribs. The pain goes up to the breast bone and is unbelievably intense. It's as if one were being sawn in two.

from the fact that the clinical explanation was perfectly plain, I must be believed when I say that I neither could nor would simulate such pain. A few months later the rumour ran around that the 'pretended' injury had been a strike against Enzo Ferrari, to force extreme demands (money and influence in the team) out of him. In all its aspects this theory is just too foolish to be worth consideration.

I saw at once that I shouldn't be able to race, the pain and the restricted movements were beyond discussion. The vultures sat around waiting. Reutemann came to my mechanics and asked, 'Well, what is it now, is he or isn't he going to drive?' They said *no,* and Reutemann went without a word to the transport where I was lying, and had a look at me. He saw that I was white and couldn't move, and he smiled, turned on his heel and went away. His face, his movements, everything expressed such evident pleasure, as if to say that one's gone, I can forget about him. I don't hold it against him, nobody expects demonstrations of sympathy, and when I hear just before an important race that Andretti has got appendicitis and can't drive I don't begin to cry. This business doesn't leave much room for sympathy . . . but all the same you can't behave quite so tactlessly as Reutemann and make the whole thing even worse than it need be. To have Reutemann for a teammate was never agreeable, not for one single second.

While in Salzburg I did concentrated work with my therapist Willy Dungl, to get myself fit once more, from Italy came the expected psychological treatment. Ferrari published in a statement to the press that Lauda was *fragile,* and that he always cracked up. And the Old Man ordered me to go to Bologna and see his own doctor, to have an overhaul. He checked me over and wrote that I had 'a well-trained body'. He gave me the scrap of paper and I showed it to the Old Man with a flourish. 'So much for your "fragile" '.

16. Technique

The mystery of that year : the cars were crazy. Not only at Ferrari's – ask Tyrrell –; but the phenomenon was worse for us and harder to explain because for two years we'd been on top. My accident, and the testing arrears which resulted from it, all that wasn't enough to explain why during this spring we were stuck fast.

It isn't only the race results which count, because they depend on so many circumstances – among others luck, bad luck – but practice times give real information as to relative strength. And they were worse than ever before. I was sixth at Monaco (a 'Ferrari circuit' !) at Zolder eleventh, in Sweden fifteenth, at Dijon ninth.

The difficulties lay to a great extent in the new tyre development. After Firestone went out and before Michelin came in our sport lived with the Goodyear monopoly of Goodyears. All the constructors had to fit out their cars with the same tyres, but with every new advance at Goodyear the individual teams got better or worse served.

We were completely wrongheaded, and my stupidity was partly to blame, I was just as wrong as Forghieri. We developed in the wrong direction and got further and further from a solution; it was the classic misunderstanding situation.

It came about because the car as it turned into the corner didn't react to the steering wheel, it under-steered then as it went into the turn it suddenly gripped at the front and began to oversteer. It was obvious that you could never drive properly in this way, and the lap times were therefore bad.

We thought at first that the under-steering was because we had too little front downforce, and that the tyres did not press hard enough on the ground, so we tried a constructive new solution with changed wings, which would push down more strongly.

We were irritated by the new Lotus, which is constructed so as to use the maximum width permitted, and with optimal down-pressure. Through even greater pressure we came to more and more modifications of the wings which only got us deeper in the muck. The races in Belgium and Sweden were the worst ever, the pressure to do better became greater, and at the same time the purely human difficulties with Forghieri got sharper.

We went on testing, on and on, until suddenly, at Dijon, we realized we were working in the wrong direction. We had already far exceeded the narrow band of optimal adhesion of the racing tyres. Optimal adhesion is only possible when the side walls of the tyres are working properly and being warmed from the inside. The tyre must to a certain extent work up to the right temperature which comes from the movement of the reinforcing threads in the carcass. Only in this way does the tyre get the best possible 'grip', and permit through its elasticity a smooth cornering. If the tyre is not warmed from the inside by hysterisis but too quickly heated from the outside it stays stiff and inelastic, and this leads to the difficulties we had halfway through the season. Through the high pressure we gave at this time to the front axle, the side walls were so strongly compressed that the tyres were simply not able to work properly.

It sounds simple today, shortly described, but at the time it was terrifically hard to find out. As soon as we had understood what was the matter we changed our whole strategy and worked in another direction. Already by the next race, at Silverstone, the Ferraris were afloat once more – from then on our cars were fundamentally okay.

With Forghieri there were, however, still difficulties, because the fundamental solution isn't everything. Every race circuit brings new questions and problems. Today the car is going badly, it's going badly here – yesterday, there, it was still going well. Why? You work with every means at your disposal from human intelligence to computer analysis, on every possible fact, but there is no absolute certainty that today's winning car will also tomorrow, on the next circuit, go well. Through the ever more highly complicated technicalities, the combination of factors like the surface of the track, corner shape, temperature, tyres, suspension and aerodynamics becomes so complicated that it is almost a mystery, and every time new and subtle methods are necessary.

Close co-operation between technicians and drivers is essential. Working with Forghieri there was always friction from hysteria and overwrought emotions. When everything is going well, when the car is going perfectly and everything works according to plan, Mauro is the most charming man, a delightful, nice colleague. But when complications arise, the work together leads to depression and friction for everyone concerned.

When in the Ferrari team everything hung in the balance, and when we needed to use every scrap of our capacities, in order to get the technical side under control and to bring the improvements to a successful conclusion, the last thing we wanted in the team was political troubles. Therefore I got into a difficult situation, because the Old Man wanted me to tell him how I envisaged the future and whether I would drive for him next year. At the same time rumours ran around that I was going to leave Ferrari's; the Italian newspapers had their usual scoops and made the Old Man mistrustful. Ferrari wanted to keep me, therefore he took it as an insult if I wished to leave. At the present moment I had to do all I could to hold together the full potential of the team – and if I said the wrong thing emotions would break through to such an extent that the whole programme would be endangered. To avoid panic was the order of the day. And there was only one way of calming them down : I promised the Old Man to drive for him as long as he lived. This was unquestionably unfair, but it was an absolute necessity; sugar for the lion.

Practice, first drive, first corner. I move the steering wheel and it doesn't do nearly enough. The car understeers wildly, then oversteers. At the back of the circuit is a succession of quick corners – always fast – only not today, not now with this car. I can't drive flat out because the car is so light in front.

I go to the pits and tell Forghieri that there's bad trouble. You can't drive with this car. Impossible, he says, you're just imagining it, look at Carlos, he's driving a second and a half faster than you, he's sixth, and where are you? I'm not trying for a time, say I, there's no point, we must first get the car right. He says so and so and I say no no no, we quarrel. The special engine, which I had, was supposed to be especially good but it goes three or four km an hour slower than normal on the straight. So I change the engine, take the old practice car, which goes badly and handles badly, I am furious. Forghieri hardly listens, he is always bad at listening. I say there is over-steer on slow corners, he makes a couple of suggestions, among them; 'I'll give you more wing at the back.' Are you mad, I say, I should get so much under-steering on the fast corners that I should be even slower overall. He began to howl. I want more wing in front, he howls some more and goes off. The time was getting short; the mechanics made the alterations I asked for. But it is just as bad, despite my stubbornness the car is no better.

Forghieri is back and bawls me out : 'Now you see, if you'd listened to me, if you'd followed me !'

We are in the middle of practice, and I say, 'What do you want to do? Thank you, here's the car, take it and do whatever you like.'

He began, changed the whole car, less wing in front, stiffer springs at the back, although we've never changed the springs all season because we know the springs are okay. Different anti shock pads, different wings and different tyres, I could hardly bear to watch. That's not how you get a solution.

The reconstruction finished, I drive away. As soon as I leave the pits, at the first steering twist, I note that nothing is improved. I drive the lap to the end and come straight back, without checking my time.

Forghieri rages : 'No lap time, no lap time,' he cries, 'it's impossible to work with you.'

I say : 'Why should I go round in two and a half minutes when all the others do it in one-fifteen?' He howls and shouts that I purposely go slow to justify myself, that I only do it to annoy him. The quarrel tires us both out, and I say, 'Please go away and let me do what I want.' It doesn't help much, the day is nearly over and I am one and a half seconds slower than Andretti – fourth row, unless something marvellous happens tomorrow.

Last practice : I took the practice car and had it modified in the way I felt it should be. In the last hour of practice it is senseless to think of further changes, now you must just step on the gas as madly as possible. It is the last consequence of racing driving, it is the deliberate overstepping of any normal limit. You must go over the kerbs that saves hundredths and tenths; scraping the kerb is part of this chaotic lap. When you drive on the kerb the car shakes to such an extent that anything may happen – with a bit of bad luck. It is then that you get the inexplicable accidents, when people say how could he have crashed into the barriers just there, how could such a thing possibly happen? A spin on a normal surface is relatively harmless and you generally work out which way you are going, have a good chance to correct and in the end brake and stop somewhere. But in these chaotic laps everything is upside down, I bang against the kerb and bang off it and the knocks are so hard and forceful that the steering column bruises my hands, and I realise that the car only holds its direction by a tiny margin, the slightest additional rumble and it would have flown off the track.

I go seven-tenths of a second quicker than the day before, so that I start in the second row : good enough.

Forghieri in the pits : 'Look, look, why is it suddenly all right, you see now the car had got nothing wrong.'

I point to my left foot and say : 'I drove like a madman, you see, but the car is no better. And really the only point of driving in such a crazy way is when all technical possibilities, all hope of modifications are exhausted. Don't you understand that ?'

But he isn't listening.

Chaotic laps worry all the drivers. They have become more frequent in recent years, because with the well-balanced line-up on the grid it has become more important which row you start from. Everyone must surpass himself three, four, five times, and forget normal drivng and out-do and over-do everything. The man himself is overwrought, he dives into another world and can't get out again just because physically he's back in the pits between times.

I study the times of my opponents, and am surprised by Scheckter's poor performance, he's only fifteenth. What's wrong with Jody, I ask a few journalists who are standing around. They reply : He's got a look in his eye as if he might lash out at anyone who came too near, or asked him anything. We don't know what's the matter, because we can't ask him.

So I go to Scheckter and say : 'What's the matter? Why won't you speak to those people?'

He says : 'Can't you understand? I drove like a pig, my nose was bleeding badly. I took every risk, and yet I'm fifteenth. What can I say when someone questions me? I could bash him or turn away. So I turn away.'

The tremendous effort of the chaotic laps is worth it, or at any rate has some sense, when you do a good time. If you are on pole position you know at least that the madness paid off. But when you've done everything and find yourself in the eighth row next to Mr Patrese, you've had enough. You know you've driven just as well as Andretti, he couldn't be cleverer than you've been, or have taken greater risks – but he's simply got the better car today, and therefore he's one and a half seconds faster. He is first and Scheckter is fifteenth, and Scheckter has the feeling that his performance was just as good.

To get out of the mood of surpassing yourself, of flying, out of the unconscious fury and disappointments, back to normal, is difficult. A few years ago in Canada I once became so savage that I hit a marshal on the head with my helmet because he was madly gesticulating and wanted to turn off the main switch on my car, which started the fire extinguisher. I was not 'back to normal' when I hit the man. I was so shocked by what had happened that whatever the circumstances I can always keep control of myself now. The mind commands the emotions.

I know exactly what makes Jody say he can't answer questions, because he is so wound up – and so full of fury, and disappointment, and tension.

17. Flying

Over the last three years flying has taken an ever more important place in my life. First I learnt to fly on small airplanes, then I got my own twin-engined Golden Eagle, then – when it had no more secrets for me – I even got a jet. I had found a way to make jet flying financially possible, by acting as promoter of Dr Polsterer's charter plane business, and in this way I got very favourable terms for a Cessna Citation. For a jet you need two pilots, I was one and the other somebody from the Polsterer crew, usually Kaar or Kemetinger.

The best example of my lust for flying : I even flew in the little Citation (places for six passengers) to California for the race at Long Beach. Flying time for the flight there 23 hours 17 minutes, but we made seven stops. We went Salzburg – Glasgow – Reykjavik – Nassarsuaqu (Greenland) – Sept Iles (Canada) – Cleveland – Kansas City – Albuquerque – Long Beach. A fair question : What happens if there's a breakdown in Greenland? But we had none, and anyway there's a certain madness in making the journey to the west coast of the United States in such a way. I thought it was grand.

I twice visited the Northrop factory in Los Angeles, and met important people, but I never got to fly one of their planes because all Northrop planes are under the Test Rules of the US Air Force, and no foreigners are allowed. It was different at the Paris Air Show at Le Bourget, where Northrop was exhibiting its models, and where they had more freedom of movement than at home. A white-haired Chief Pilot took me with him in a two seater F5 supersonic fighter bomber.

The nonchalance of the announcement, when he asks the control tower permission for a supersonic flight : Paris control, request supersonic ride, as if you were fetching the milk, but for security ask permission. The flight itself is abstract; he says nose down, I put the nose down and notice nothing special, you only see the speed when you look at the instrument board : faster than sound, and a bit more, make 1.4, fine. The Chief does a few supersonic tricks, but acrobatics don't interest me, sub-sonic or supersonic I feel scared and also rather silly. It all goes so fast that I can't think, and I can't coordinate what the pilot does with what the airplane does, and therefore all that remains is a sort of circus effect with ohs and ahs. So I say, enough, enough, I only want to fly normally without anything artificial.

I fly beautifully around, make lovely circles above the sea, then the pilot got a Jumbo on his radar screen, and he said if he'd been armed . . . and then he said there was *one* thing he must show me, I must see it, no backing out. Between two banks of cloud he put the airplane into a vertical flight, we go straight up into the sky. Going straight upwards is slower, the push of the machine stops. I can see how the speed diminishes. The pilot is above me, beneath me is Paris, and the speed gets less and less. The transmission gets quieter and quieter and quieter, in the earphones the pilot's breathing is heard, ahh-fff, abb-fff (in, out) otherwise silence; his breathing is now much the loudest noise. I naturally realize that it's a critical moment when you fly too slowly, he may lose balance and go into a spin. 100 knots, 70, 60, 50, 40 and the pilot sits exactly above me and breathes in the earphones, in and out, in and out, it is frightfully unpleasant, I hang in my seat belt and don't know what will happen next.

Finally we have nought on the speedometer, we are staying still in the air.

'Look,' says he, 'zero speed.'

I shout : 'And now?' and he says softly : 'I put the nose down gently,' and in fact he slowly puts the nose down, the plane never loses balance, or spins in the slightest, the nose points down and now I'm above the pilot and I can see Paris, he still gives no gas, then we accelerate slowly. Another time I would laugh at it, and find it amusing, but the first time I was afraid. Not knowing what will happen next is disagreeable. I fly back, make the whole ILS, he does the landing.

18. Opponents

A modest fifth place at Dijon put me in the lead for the world championship – more or less by chance, because the opposition was so split up, had break-downs and made mistakes. After the next race – second at Silverstone – with our much-improved car I had the thing in the bag. Then came the lovely victory at Hockenheim, one year after the accident. Second at the Oesterreich-Ring and a win at Zandvoort put the opponents further behind, I was as good as World Champion. There were three potential winners this year : Andretti, Hunt, Scheckter, in that order.

Mario Andretti had the best hope because he had the best car of the year. When everything goes right with a Lotus there's nothing better. But the car wasn't reliable enough. It had engine breakdowns which can perhaps be laid at the door of a too experimental engine, but again perhaps not (you get breakdowns often enough with normal machines) and then Mario himself made mistakes. When somebody is one and a half seconds faster in practice than the next fastest (Zolder), you shouldn't react to a bad start so that you are straightaway in a collision. With this, he threw away the biggest superiority any driver had in any race this year. And at Zandvoort he had another collision, with Hunt.

If Andretti was my strongest opponent as far as the car went, Hunt had the greatest driving potential. By and large he was the best driver of the season. I can't remember him making a single mistake, and therefore it's hard to judge why things went wrong for him. Possibly at the beginning of the season he was too content to rest on his laurels as World Champion, or perhaps it just didn't happen, without anyone being able to give an exact reason for it. In any case James is still for me the most dangerous opponent.

Jody Scheckter was also uncannily good in 1977, no question. He had the handicap of winning right away with a new team and a new car, a hard thing to deal with. To come up from nothing and straight off to be first makes quite a difficult situation. Then came mistakes, no doubt, some technical and some that he himself made. From one minute to the next the car didn't go right, and nobody knew why, the situation was partly the same as Tyrrell's or even Ferrari's. His own faults: a pile-up in Sweden, a missed tyre change at Zolder, an impatient and unnecessary lapping of an opponent at Zeltweg which ended with him going off the road. He could just as easily have overtaken three laps later, it wouldn't have mattered at all.

These three – Andretti, Hunt, Scheckter – were genuine opponents this year. Over Reutemann I never worried.

I have been describing other people's mistakes; what about my own? I made a hash of the start at Long Beach and wasn't in top form there; I drove a bad race in Sweden, not that it made much difference because the car was hopelessly inferior. Otherwise I have nothing to reproach myself with. Looking back in this way, and judging what happened you must take into account the actual situation. There are things which seem to have been mistakes, but as things were at the time were not mistakes at all. Of course I could have won at Zeltweg if I had foreseen exactly what the weather would be – but that's too hypothetical.

19. Giving Notice

The date of the win at Zandvoort suited my plan for giving notice splendidly. I wanted straight away, after the victory, to make it clear that I wouldn't make another contract with Ferrari, because once again it wouldn't suit their scheme of things. A win, practically World Champion, more on top than ever – and even so the fellow wants to leave? Four years of *pressure* are enough, four years of blowing hot and cold are the maximum. One couldn't blame the Old Man for all this. An ancient monumental personality with iron principles, a Commendatore Enzo Ferrari, must be accepted as he is, otherwise you couldn't stick as much as a single month in the firm. If that had been all, well and good. Despite all his peculiarities I really would have stayed with the Old Man for the rest of his life, as I promised him, when once again chaos broke out and I had to use every means to bring peace to the team.

But the domination of the Old Man along with the unpredictability of the Ferrari underground and the spikiness of Mauro Forghieri – all that was too much for a fifth year. Perhaps Forghieri was the determining factor of the three, in building up so much *pressure* in the team. He believed so firmly in himself and his ideas that he forced them through regardless of everything. It is perfectly normal that a driver should long to have a technician who doesn't make a tragic drama out of every testing session, but who will cooperate coolly and realistically in their work together. But I must stress once again that I do believe in Mauro Forghieri. The man's a genius. My bad luck, that I can't get on with geniuses.

To explain all this to the Old Man is senseless; he would never accept it and would always assume that there must be other reasons. This is based on our relatively simple relations to one another. He only remembers that he has treated me 'like a son', and to be betrayed by a son – how mean, to leave him just when his driver is at the peak of their achievement together. The way he had treated me after Fuji he had most likely completely forgotten. That he had made his mind up to drop me, to make me into a 'team manager' doubtless never occurred to him now, as he looked back .It was therefore senseless to argue with the Commendatore with the slightest hope of success, once he was on the theme of 'ungratefulness' and 'betrayal'; of the Judas who sold himself for thirty sausages.

Immediately after giving notice I flew to Turin. That evening I met Giovanni and Umberto Agnelli, in order to take farewell of the Fiat business. I told them the way I saw things, and the reasons I had, and they accepted them. We had a straightforward good relationship.

After a few days I had to go to the first practice at Monza, where the Italian Grand Prix was fixed for twelve days later. Of course it would have been more diplomatic to have given notice after the Monza race, but I didn't give much for diplomacy, I could easily get through the days at Monza, I didn't worry. To imagine that Ferrari would take some sort of revenge would have seemed to me absurd.

When I came to the routine tests I was completely relaxed, pleased that I had given notice, happy to think that a new future lay before me. There were unusually many people at Monza, considering the relative unimportance of the occasion. On the roof of the pits lay a couple of fans, one of them crazily began to insult Ferrari, saying, 'Without Lauda you're going to have a thin time' and Forghieri looked up horrified; others shouted that it was high time that Lauda left. The atmosphere made you wonder what would happen at the Grand Prix.

Italian journalists crowded round me, they obviously couldn't get over my having given notice and they sought an explanation. They pressed closer and closer until they had me in a ring and I must speak and answer. Probably because I was so pleased that everything had been cleared up, I was particularly straight in my answers, but not just dry statements, I couldn't resist teasing them.

When they persistently asked me, 'Why?' I spoke to an old journalist. I asked how long he'd been married, he said forty years. I asked him if his wife was still beautiful, had she still got a good figure? He looked embarrassed and said, no. Then I asked him whether he still loved her all the same, and he said yes. Okay, says I, you love her, that's fine. But supposing you didn't love her, would it help if she strapped up her bosom and had her face lifted? No, says he, it wouldn't make any difference. There you are, I said, that's how it is with my love for Ferrari. When there's no more love it has nothing to do with outward things. That's why it wouldn't help a bit if they changed a lot, it would only be a face lift, it wouldn't make me happy.

I don't know why I thought of such a comparison, it would have been cleverer not to give it. The whole thing was completely distorted by the newspapers, and went in its distorted form right through the international agencies, in any case I paid for it, even in Germany. They said I was vulgar and that I treated women like muck. My whole comparison was shortened and the papers said that I'd said : 'When a woman gets older and loses her figure I leave her.' I don't know whether they purposely misquoted me or whether my poor Italian was to blame for the mistranslation. As an example, here is a typical letter I got from Germany :

Herr Lauda,

I am an Austrian, married in Bavaria. Since a few weeks I have been following your interviews in the German papers. And I must say, that as an Austrian I am ashamed of my compatriot. 'Think of the relationship between a man and his wife, that has lasted many years. The wife goes physically downhill, her bosom gets slack, so love dies.' (TZ of the 1 September 1977.)

If for you the relationship of husband and wife only rests on physical beauty, a full bosom and a perfect figure, then one knows what sort of a man you are. If your wife, who is so pretty and young, should have children, does your love for her stop at that moment. Pregnancy often changes a woman's body for the worse (and I don't mean her carelessness.) By your way of thinking you should be glad day and night that your wife is still with you, for you were never handsome, and since your accident . . . well.

If I compare you with a slack bosom I must say in your case love will have stopped at your face. It is a sad thing for a man to express himself in such a way. I never liked you much. But since I have heard some of your opinions I find you conceited and overbearing. Already 90% of the population can't stand you. It would be funny if you could get rid of the other 10% as well. It always hurts me when people devaluate the idea of an Austrian by using the term in connection with you. You are certainly not a good advertisement for our country abroad. I have never written a letter like this before, because I am far too busy for such amusements, but these statements of yours have made all my friends and acquaintances so furious, and I as an Austrian couldn't say anything.

Birgit Reiter, 8233 Aufham.

This obviously genuine letter is an example which shows how helpless a public figure is against misquotation and manipulation. Any journalist can tear things out of context, slant them, and get a statement which is the opposite of the truth. I can do nothing, and hundreds of thousands of people just think Lauda is a swine. It's not a case of the few hundred who write angry letters, – they can be answered, so long as they give an address – but the majority get the false impression and I can do nothing about it. Therefore up to a point I don't care what people think of me, because if I did I should have to sit in a corner and cry. Ought I to call a press conference and say: 'That thing about the slack bosom, I meant it quite differently;' should I send out a statement: 'Lauda is not a computer, he's not a machine, he's not cold, not brutal?' This is a fight you can't win, so I must accept that people see me as the publicity people like to show me.

The thought of the race at Monza didn't worry me in the slightest. Some people would no doubt treat me as an enemy, the atmosphere in the team might not be very grand, but after all the scenes I had gone through it would be a bagatelle. Only the chance that some madman might make the headlines by sticking a knife into me was slightly more likely than usual because of the attacks in the Italian press. Therefore I suggested to Ghedini that it might not be a bad idea to organize two or three bodyguards, just for the times when I was in the crowds. I didn't want a kick in the behind, not to speak of worse, and Ghedini completely saw my point. At Monza there's always gigantic chaos, it's not to be compared with any other race in the world. My idea was to keep clear of the chaos as far as possible, otherwise nerves go to pieces.

For choice of where to stay it's not necessary to be near the racecourse. What counts is peace and quiet and seclusion. So I stay with Marlene at the Villa d'Este on Lake Como, and Walter Wolf's helicopter takes me to and fro. Fifth place in practice, okay. Once I crashed into the barriers, because I had forgotten that I had cold tyres. Unbelievable, an old hand like me making such a mistake.

Before the race I asked our green team manager whether there were any orders, I just want to know whether I must drive against Jody Scheckter (my only remaining challenger for the world championship) or whether I also had to fight my colleague in the team, Reutemann.

Nosetto says : 'We want to win the championship as much as you do, it's just as important for Ferrari.'

Fine, and to be sure I say again : 'That means that Reutemann is on my side in the race?'

Yes, says Nosetto, green as usual.

In the early morning I practised starts and was quite impressed at how splendidly they went. You recognize a super-start by a certain tyre vibration, the tyres have got so much grip. You can only do two of those trial starts, otherwise the car suffers. At the trial starts I got 9500 revolutions, and I got the same in the race, but like a fool I'd forgotten that the car was heavier now. This morning I only had 150 litres of petrol and now I've got 180, and the whole calculation with the 9500 revolutions is no longer correct, and I choke the motor and don't get away so perfectly. I get behind Reutemann, lying fifth or sixth. The competition gets faster, and I notice how Reutemann pulls three or four lengths away from me everytime in the straight, so obviously today he's got the stronger engine. As long as he makes no mistake I've no chance of overtaking him, but he will help me, according to the team rules – or?

We are now lying second and third, out in front is Andretti, now it would naturally be the moment for him to let me by. I wait for a signal from the pits; nothing. I am irritated, because I don't know what he's up to. It would be madness to risk attacking him, if he has really planned to let me go past anyway.

More and more I get the feeling that I must expect nothing from him – except a fight to the finish. I see Carlos losing an exhaust pipe, I can't get out of the way but nothing is damaged. Reutemann's engine has lost power, that is obvious, and I have no problem about passing him now.

I see the surface of the track is shining, oil! I make a quick twist to the left and can brake for the chicane on the dry line – no problem. I look in the mirror and see nothing – where is my Argentine friend? He had chosen to stop, keeping to his same line, rather than to brake on the oil patch.

I've got slight understeer, nothing much, but enough so that there's no hope of catching Andretti. He is unbeatable today; I am second, getting six points – practically World Champion. The journey home is already planned : as quick as possible out of the chaos, bodyguards, helicopter, Linate, the Citation; at half past six I'm in Salzburg. On the car radio I hear our green Nosetto giving an interview. Had there been any sort of stable orders for the Ferraris, the reporter wants to know.

'No, there was no arrangement,' said Nosetto, 'because we have two intelligent drivers.'

Well, there you have an abridged version of all the Ferrari problems, the tortuous ways in the underground. I didn't demand an arrangement, I simply wanted to know whether there was one. The team manager tells the driver there's a team order, but there wasn't one. What did he say to Reute-mann? Would he have let me pass in the last lap, or would he have said serves you right? I shall never know.

20. The Boxer

The Italian newspapers hotted up the Ferrari people against me. As a result the Old Man became ever more furious in his comments, and the hoped-for smooth parting became impossible. Team-coordinator Sante Ghedini, who was pro-Lauda, was suddenly fired. His only crime had been that he stood by me.

When I was at Maranello for the usual routine test before Watkins Glen, I happened to run into the Commendatore. He shouted at me, hadn't I the courage to shake hands? Yes, of course, naturally, I said, and held out my hand. He shouted that it was monstrous the way I tried to get his staff away from him. As far as my chief mechanic Ermanno Cuoghi goes, I admit I wanted to persuade him to leave, but Cuoghi was still hesitating; he loved Ferrari, and also he needed security for his family and was nervous at the idea of going to live in England. I had had nothing to do with Ghedini. Although I value him greatly as a person, I had never made him any offer, I had no job for him. I told Enzo Ferrari this, and I added that he could be sure in the present situation I should very much like to find a job for Ghedini . . . in fact I should be grateful that he'd fired Ghedini, an important thing for me.

The Old Man was so utterly furious that he went around shouting nonsense, whereupon I began to shout too. It ended with him screaming that 'except for work' I should never be allowed to set foot on the estate again, and while he was in the midst of his tirade I seized his hand, shook it, said *Arrivederci,* turned on my heel and left him standing there shouting. I felt sorry for him at that moment, as he stood surrounded by his people, helplessly foaming at the mouth. He was simply too old, he didn't understand the circumstances any more, or see how things were; he just felt he'd been attacked for no reason. Why must all these emotions build up, why must so much china be smashed, why couldn't they accept the end of my contract with them according to the normal rules of European business life? It was enough to make you weep. After four years of work together there was, in spite of differences of opinion, a common denominator of our successes together, and then in a few days everything was trampled underfoot, just as though the partnership had been a failure from beginning to end, the whole four years.

I knew at that time already that I should go to Brabham. Sorting out the possibilities during the whole year gave the following picture : There were four top teams – Lotus, McLaren, Wolf and Brabham. Lotus there was no question of, for me; I am simply not the right type for the team, for some reason I can't explain. McLaren would have been a perfect team, with good, clever people, a good organization and good cars. But a combination James Hunt/Niki Lauda wouldn't work in the long run; Hunt's position in the team was too dominant. That left Wolf and Brabham. I get on marvellously with Walter Wolf, and he would have liked to take me, but basically I had less confidence in the Wolf car than in the Brabham/Alfa, especially the new model which was being tried out in Autumn 1977. I had agreed with the team manager Bernie Ecclestone, but we had to wait to sign up until we were sure of the chief sponsor for the team – the Italian dairy business Parmalat. There was a public relations job for Ghedini, so he will stay with me in the same way as before.

With Cuoghi it was more complicated. I wanted to take him, but he found the decision difficult. During all these four years Cuoghi had been my personal chief mechanic, who was directly responsible for my car. He had six mechanics under him, three of whom in turns were at the races. Under his leadership from 1974 till 1977 there were only three examples of carelessness, and none of them in the actual races. At practice in Watkins Glen two years ago the bolt holding the shock absorber was not done up, the shock absorber jumped out, the car almost got away from me and I very nearly went off. At practice in Mosport the crew once forgot to tighten the right hand back wheel, which worked loose, and then in 1977 in practice at Zeltweg they forgot to see to the water system. Only three mistakes in sixty races and hundreds of tests and practices, that is super.

Cuoghi wanted time to think it over; he said he would tell me after the USA and Canadian races. Okay.

I flew to Los Angeles and tried to get the next stage of my pilot's licence, although it was not quite clear how far American exams would count in Europe. Apart from that I waited in vain for the exam result, with the analysis which the computer was supposed to spit out.

Marlene and I flew back to New York where the illustrated paper *Bunte* had arranged a meeting between me and Mohammed Ali. For the newspaper people this was a photo scoop, and I liked the idea because Clay interests me. It was just two days before his title fight with Ernie Shavers, and he was to await me in his suite at the New York Statler Hilton.

A manager, a normal man. Otherwise odd types, the bodyguards and people going in and out. I had to wait a quarter of an hour outside the door. Then I go into another room, next to his bedroom, and wait again. I go in, the room is almost dark; Clay is lying in bed, the blankets pulled up to his shoulders. A woman sits by the bed; he says in my direction, 'Wait a second', very slowly. After a couple of minutes the woman gets a hint to go away, I am taken to the bed and sit beside him. No smile, he just lies there, dull and apathetic and speaks very slowly, in flat, bored tones. Photos are taken.

'You are the greatest in racing,' he announces. 'I am the greatest in boxing' and then he drawls, 'But I am greater, I am the greatest in the whole wide world.'

It's more annoying than in the cinema; what is play-acting, what is real? Is he in a trance? There lies a stolid, goggle-eyed man in bed and brings out the silliest commonplaces. Is it part of the show or – electrifying thought – is it real?

The audience lasted about a quarter of an hour; I was puzzled. I didn't know what to make of so much stupidity, so much arrogance, such a degree of silliness. With all the famous sportsmen I have met there has always been one rule, as a matter of course : you don't put on a show for each other. We can all put on a show, and sometimes we have to in public – but for heaven's sake not with one another. To play-act for another sportsman would be grotesque. We all know the rules of the money-making game, we also know the disadvantages; for example, having no time, or wanting to be left in peace. Everyone has the same problems. If I say to Franz Klammer, look, I've no time for you at the moment, he knows exactly what I mean; there are times when I should be a nuisance to him. Among all the big-time boys I have ever met, Ali is the only one who completely lives in his pretence world, and did his act in front of me, as it were from over there. Even that idea is more comforting than the thought that the whole thing may be real, and that Ali is really as stupid and arrogant and apathetic as he seems.

Watkins Glen, the American Grand Prix : I only need one single point, and I'm World Champion for 1977. Therefore

I shall drive 'tactically', because I naturally want the world championship all sewn up and in the bag.

I fly from the Glen Motor Inn in the helicopter and land on the circuit. A journalist says, 'Have you heard, they've sacked Cuoghi.' It makes me feel sick, I must pull myself together : That can't be true! How far will the hatred of the Ferrari people go?

The reconstruction of what happened was this : Cuoghi was rung up in the night Saturday/Sunday by Ferrari and asked whether he was staying on with Ferrari or going with me. Cuoghi answered he liked being at Ferrari's, but he couldn't yet decide, he must consult with his wife. They gave him time to telephone his wife, but she couldn't help him come to a decision. So he told Ferrari he was still considering his decision. 'The decision is taken,' he was told, 'you're fired.' At the same time he was forbidden to do anything more for my car; he could look upon himself as a tourist who had nothing to do with Ferrari. Cuoghi came straight to me early that morning on the race course and cried on my shoulder. The man was completely done up. What madness, to treat a man who had been a fanatical worker for Ferrari for many years, a real 'Ferrari-man', in such a way. To humiliate him, and to attack both him and me!

I forced myself with all my strength to concentrate on the race. It is awful to race when you are under psychological pressure. The mere sight of Nosetto's face stops me, sends my accelerator foot to sleep. Another 'political' drive, and I am determined to finish up the world championship business. I shall have more room to manoeuvre when that is out of the way.

It was a commonplace race, the only excitement was that the soaking wet track got drier and drier, so much so that although I didn't make a tyre change, the wet weather tyres were dangerously strained. I knew that my left hand front tyre was on its way out. All the same, a relatively easy fourth place. I am World Champion. The usual milling crowd. The mechanics congratulate me, Cuoghi is also there, we embrace – he had a big share in this title, he was *my* man, not only this year. Nosetto didn't congratulate me, it wasn't necessary.

I was hoisted on the platform, to pose with Hunt, the winner of the race. They made a way through the crowds to the Goodyear tent for the official world championship photograph. Then to the caravan, journalists, congratulations. I feel empty, because the Ferrari problem is hanging over me, the Cuoghi business, this ever more hostile attitude towards me. I've no idea what the next weeks will bring. Cuoghi says he will fly straight home and ask the Commendatore to see him, and then persuade him to allow that he looks after my car in Canada and Japan. He persuaded himself that the Old Man would agree to this. I don't contradict him, but at bottom we all know there's nothing more to be done, Cuoghi is finished as far as Ferrari goes. Out of the bustle and fuss I run to the helicopter which takes us over to the Glen Motor Inn. The world championship continued in what is known as the smallest circle. It consisted of Marlene and me.

Awaking next day : Good morning World Champion ! At the moment it doesn't mean much to me, because my second world championship is not really finished off as long as the Ferrari question isn't settled. Normally one could say : Fine, that's done, I've collected enough points – from the Oester-reich Ring on I have really only gone after the world championship in a 'political' way – and now, gentlemen, I can really step on the gas. But how can I tussle with Andretti in Canada and Japan if my own team is chaotic, without my chief mechanic, when everything is unclear ? Who practises with which car ? What role does Villeneuve play, Ferrari's new man for 1978? What a mistake, to put him in already; with three cars the team will be hopeless. The Ferrari people say he must get ready for 1978. Well, in that case it would be the proper thing for me to get ready for 1978 with Brabham; or not? I can see no solution at the moment, I only know that the Ferrari contract runs until 31st October. At present I must just wait, and think it over, but not here in the pouring rain of Watkins Glen, but right over there in Canada, where next Sunday the race takes place at Mosport. Marlene and I leave early and drive in our Fiat over the frontier. Just before Niagara Marlene gets hungry, so we have to leave the Highway and drive into the town for something to eat. We make a short detour and miss Niagara Falls. I am a terribly bad sight-seer. The same afternoon we get to the Holiday Inn at Oshawa.

Waiting, and driving around, I come to the conclusion that I am the right man in the wrong place. I simply cannot imagine that the two remaining races will be reasonable, yet on the other hand I naturally have a duty towards Ferrari, and the organizers, and the public in Canada and Japan. The World Champion, I thought, can't just give up, just because he's not enjoying himself. On the other hand the World Champion must step on the gas, he can't just dawdle round. But how can I fight, in the midst of this chaotic team?

Tuesday: Already in Europe I had promised the sponsors of the Canadian Grand Prix, the Labat Brewery, that I would 'belong' to them for a whole day, and be at the disposition of the company. That is a typical kind of promotion in America, I did it in New York too. The Canadians offered 3000 dollars, but I refused. I wouldn't do such a day under 5000 dollars. They wanted to bargain, but I did nothing until a telex came: Yes, okay then. A girl fetched me early, drove me to Toronto and put me in a suite at the Sheraton Hotel. There is an exact time schedule, every quarter of an hour another journalist, or a group of journalists, without a moment's pause.

Halfway through a buffet lunch was brought in. During lunch there are mostly TV people, it seems to me. Most of the questions grate on the nerves, and the payment for such a day I look upon as payment for the effort it costs me to go through with it. Half way I ask for the PR girl to show me the cheque, to give me strength to go on. At one moment some French journalists turn up, men I know already. It does good to get a few sensible questions for a change instead of the usual bla-bla. We had a splendid discussion and I think they went off satisfied. At the end the PR manageress is also satisfied and carts me back home – fine, it is nice to have given satisfaction.

Wednesday: Ferrari, Renault and one or two other racing stables practise at Mosport. In between comes the news that Ferrari is flying in one more car and two mechanics, they want to give me full service, I am to have priority and Villeneuve will only be sent to the start if a car remains over for him. My mood doesn't improve much, the situation is simply too muddled. I go to this half-hearted practice, where at first only the Renault is going round, then bad weather intervenes; I drive back home. I haven't even met Villeneuve, Ferrari's new man.

Thursday: I hang around at the Holiday Inn, don't know what to be at, consider this and that. Journalists who catch me on this day are in luck. On no other day in the year have I had so much time on my hands. A woman journalist from the French *Auto Hebdo* goes beyond what is permissible. She can only speak French so we need an English person to translate; he soon goes off, the questions are so painful. She asks about my sex-life, whether I get on with groupies, does it amuse me and how often do I do it? I ask myself, what is the difference between Lauda and anyone else, and whether she would have the cheek to ask other married people such questions. I give her my answers, and say please may I ask her a question, which is: do you do it much, do you enjoy it? and how many times in the last week? The translator was embarrassed and talked round the subject, but I tell him not to be cowardly, then he translated it, and she goes red and embarrassed and laughs in a silly way and gives no answer.

So I ask her: 'Why do you put questions to Lauda that you yourself refuse to answer, because you find them painful and indiscreet? Why have you got two standards?'

She doesn't answer, and goes off with an embarrassed laugh.

Friday: At seven everything becomes clear. I have got gastric flu. With gastric flu you can't drive in a race. I ring Nosetto and tell him: 'I'm not going to drive.' He says okay and rings back a few minutes later: he speaks Italian and says they are giving a statement to the press, in which it declares that I have had the best equipment, and that Villeneuve was only to drive if that in no way impaired my own action. Fine, I said, you can say that, I've nothing against it. Marlene hears the decision, gives up an excursion and by ten we are already in the car and twenty minutes later in the Lear-jet. In spite of the gastric flu I manage to visit the Lear Works at Wichita, then New York, then Swissair to Zürich, and there is the little jet. We fly to Salzburg. I sleep in the afternoon.

Everything is over, over, over. We go out in the evening, life is easy, at least for a few hours. We get home at six in the morning, I push the KTM out and drive over the fields. Then I send a telegram to Ferrari:

FOR MEDICAL REASONS UNABLE TO DRIVE IN CANADA. I THANK YOU FOR ALL THE EFFORTS THAT HAVE MADE IT POSSIBLE FOR ME TO WIN THE WORLD CHAMPIONSHIP A SECOND TIME — NIKI LAUDA.

PART
TWO

For Part One of this book Niki Lauda made many tape recordings. We then wove them together and discussed and corrected them. One thing seemed to be missing: a second point of view. Many of Lauda's commentaries and observations did not fit into the mainstream of his vision of what happened, and then some of the foregone conclusions need to be put in perspective and supplemented by an outside observer, who could question, think aloud and stand aside from all disputes.

We made this second part together, but with me as narrator.

HERBERT VÖLKER

1. The Knight's Move

Lauda needed no outside pressure, to give his journey the look of a hurried departure. His schedule was hectic, no unnecessary minutes were allowed to interfere with the target, and he scared his satellites one after another. By chance a woman photographer happened to be outside the Holiday Inn at Oshawa when Niki was loading up the Fiat; an all-inclusive *'Ciao'* for the few bystanders, a friendly grin as he drove away, the Lauda and Ferrari four-year show didn't have a very impressive finale.

Only three or four journalists from the Lauda inner circle had got wind of it; one of them grumbled : 'One can't leave him alone for a couple of hours without everything being upside down.' True : there were changes all the time. Lauda had only been four and a half days in a rather ordinary Canadian hotel, wandering around, getting in his own way, neither fish nor flesh, and when the people round him were at last certain that a decision would be announced on Saturday, he gets on the telephone at seven on Friday morning and says, 'I won't drive.'

The next three hours were concentrated action. Four and a half days he gave to thinking things out, but once the decision was taken it was a quick-motion picture. He gave himself 180 minutes for everything: the statement for Ferrari's, the briefing of the most important journalists, organizing a Lear jet to fly him to New York, arranging a visit to the

Lear factory, getting Marlene to hurry with her hush-hush packing, as counterpoint to the laziness of the past days, reserving a booking from New York to Europe, ordering his little jet to be at Zürich, packing, breakfast, paying the bill and away to the airport at Peterborough where the first Lear was waiting. Lauda flies away, leaving the Grand Prix without the star, leaving a dozen Ferrari men with grim faces going about the automatic tasks before the first practice, because Lauda or no Lauda the show must go on, only more subdued and colourless, and the bystanders go to where Hunt and Andretti are in the pits.

By chance – quite by chance – Lauda had caught the *right* day to go – a day which was perfect for getting away as far as possible. The track is awful, the organization hopeless, delay follows delay, one after another cracks up, then Ian Ashley's Hesketh leaps in the air, flies over the barriers, mows down a TV platform and Ashley lies for twenty minutes in the wreck before they manage to cut away the metal from his body. The Ferraris, driven by Reutemann and the new man Villeneuve, are twelfth and seventeenth respectively in practice, and Villeneuve goes off the track. Those left behind have the feeling once again that Lauda is impossible to classify. A knight's move was in the pattern of things, and quite to be expected, but it came at a surprising moment and with a surprising statement, so to speak planned, yet carried out in the heat of passion.

None of the stages in Lauda's life fit into a pattern; it is as though unpredictability was his system. The way he was the first racing driver to get into Formula I on borrowed money, the way he won and the way he gave up, the way he was buried by a tractor, the way he was half burnt and how and when he made his comeback, the way he married, the way he gave notice and the way he left, all this has nothing to do with the way you regulate your life, or I mine.

Racing drivers are fond of saying that they *have to be* 'different', like artists who pride themselves on the *inevitability* of not fitting in with the normal scheme of things. Friction with the average person is thus a logical consequence. Ken Purdy, biographer of Stirling Moss, takes as his motto 'Greatness doesn't come cheap'. This means: You can't make an omelette without breaking eggs.

2. A mental zip fastener

The interpretation of racing drivers' motivation.

I threw Niki a quotation. It was from Denis Jenkinson, one of the most famous of motor sport's journalists, and it dated from 1958. '. . . and over and over again I came to the conclusion that through the effects of speed, noise, and the knowledge that they are exposed to danger, some strange inner need is satisfied.'

Lauda did not think for long about this. ' "Some strange inner need is satisfied" – that's very pompously expressed. I like motor racing, and I can't separate that from an inner need or any other need, I can't say I have got such and such a feeling in my brain, another in my penis and yet another in my behind.

'As to the effect of speed and noise and danger as Jenkinson sees it; noise we can never eliminate, it certainly doesn't satisfy anything in me. The speed business is more complicated. Jenkinson wrote that twenty years ago, and at that time racing cars looked completely different and certainly gave a different feeling of speed from what we have today. The "effect" of speed on the driver in those days I don't know, I can only say that now the effect is zero. Formula I cars are built for speed. If you drive a Mercedes and a Volkswagen beetle at the same speed of 130, you get much less feeling of going fast in the Mercedes than you do in the beetle. This disappearance of the feeling of speed is ten times more pronounced in a Grand Prix car than it is in the Mercedes, because the Formula I car is constructed to go at 300. A speed which would feel sensational in an ordinary car is nothing in a Grand Prix car, not in the least exciting (and then you've got your helmet and visor as well!)

'I know that I don't "feel" the speed because I can't tell whether I'm going at 150 or 250. If someone asks me at what speed I was going at this or that position I have to think back to what revolutions I had, then I look at the translation sheet: 12,000 revolutions, that makes 280 kilometres an hour. On the straight – the only place where you get the highest speed – the modern Grand Prix cars lie in such a way that the car "does" nothing, it isn't lighter, it doesn't "move".

'Even the corners don't give any special feeling. There is of course the centrifugal force which presses on your head, but it makes no difference whether I take a sharp corner at 150 or a long bend at 250.

'Acceleration? Yes, it was a thrill when I sat in the March the first three minutes and for the first time felt almost 500 horse power. But after a time you don't feel anything special at the acceleration.

'Imagine if you really felt a thrill racing; you'd get a centrifugal force orgasm on corners, a speed orgasm on the straight, you would go from one emotion to another and with so many thrills you wouldn't be able to drive at all. People whose "needs are satisfied" are wankers, but not racing drivers.

'As to being satisfied by the knowledge of being "exposed to danger", I can guarantee that for me that isn't so. Consciousness of danger is naturally there, but that's not the point. The decision whether to race in spite of the danger you make once and then *basta,* you can't keep asking yourself the same question on every corner. Although the question is so to speak put on one side, it remains of course a certain strain on you. Only a masochist would find that agreeable.'

VÖLKER : 'Okay, but then what do you get out of racing? Surely not just the money?'

LAUDA : 'I get joy out of the fascination with perfection, not from the thrill of motor racing. For example, a lap where in every respect everything goes right, every single manoeuvre – that sort of lap is marvellous, it gives satisfaction. And when the time check shows you were really good, you feel happy.'

VÖLKER : 'That sounds a bit like a complete cliché, but surely this feeling can't just be that. Describe what a success is really like.'

LAUDA : 'You've got to imagine how the pressure has built up, harder and harder, because time has gone by and we've had practice and the others have got very good practice times, while I've been working mostly at the adjustment of the car. And I know I must soon do something, something's got to happen, and the pressure gets harder all the time. I get into the car and drive three laps, to warm up the tyres. While I'm doing that I concentrate hard on the *now or never, and then let's go – with everything I've got.* All the same this lap isn't optimal, I register some small mistake, see where I could brake a second later; another lap, but then I'm too fast into the corner and come out with the car across the track, and know I made a hash of it, so one more lap, the last, because you can't drive longer in this way : so, pull yourself together, don't go crooked, don't do anything silly, brake later, do the maximum. And after each corner you feel rather pleased, because it went so perfectly, ah, here comes the bend where you made a mistake, but now it's right, I come into it beautifully, drift to the kerb, graze it so that I can hardly hold the car, but I step on the gas, couldn't have gone better and I've saved the tenth of a second. And when all the other corners go the same you might as well go back to the pits. That's it, thank you, gentlemen, everything is all right, it won't go faster than that, that's the best I shall do this practice, I can't start all over again. The satisfaction at that moment is enormous, and when they confirm my time, 39 and thirty two, I lapped in 1.39.32, then I sit down and am happy and do nothing more, even though there's half an hour more practice. What's the matter, asks Forghieri, whatever's wrong? Nothing, say I, I can't go faster, and if the others drive faster today I'm sorry, the others are just faster that's all. But nobody does such a good time and I sit quietly there and watch and I'm a happy man.

Bullfighters and racing drivers are always the most highly valued objects when it's a question of mind and soul and motivation. Lauda has become quite accustomed to clever people who like to try and find out about his super-ego, or his hidden ego, or his repressions. Although he thinks it's rubbish he patiently cooperates, and undoes his mental zip fastener.

Hildegard Knef in the *Bunte Illustrierte* defines the statement of the problem in relentless super-kitsch :

'His smile is broad, although his mouth is small. His eyes are kind and seemingly guileless. He radiates an attractive, manly, sometimes rather touching personality.

Somewhere in his eyes there is a gleam of humour. They are large, wide, light in colour.

Where is the mainspring hidden, which scares him in the child-sized car – which drives him into the deadly dangerous game? I have no idea. Shocks in childhood? The need to show off? Impossible to say.'

Peter Handke came to the gloomiest conclusion about Lauda's attitude to his inner life. The description dates from the year 1975, when Handke interviewed Lauda for *Der Spiegel*. His girl-friend Mariella was a great admirer of Handke's books, and Lauda was quite pleased to place himself at Handke's disposal, even at Nürburgring among all the hurry and fuss, because the poet wanted to make a study in depth and to get to know the motor racing world.

Niki was curious to see the result, rather like somebody who had been on Freud's couch to be analysed. Lauda should have had his doubts, because when discussing what his impressions of the first race of his life had been, Handke suggested he felt as if he was in an hotel bedroom where he could hear the sexual act being performed next door. Then it was clear to Lauda that he, Niki, saw his sport in too simple a fashion, because in all the years he had been motor racing he had never thought of the sexual act or of the complicated idea of the acoustics next door.

In his *Spiegel* article Handke didn't mention sex. Instead he described Lauda as a man who only lived with a troupe of technicians, and with joyless, stupid professionals. Handke had observed the technicians excellently but too superficially, and he pretended to be astonished at their technical language (in other words motor racing slang) as though he had fallen asleep in 1900 and now suddenly woke up in the grand stand. Handke annihilated the crowd of spectators : '. . . at the Nürburgring, the two hundred thousand tragically unreal beer-swillers with their empty lives and women with taciturn expressions, as if they were all just back from a punitive expedition . . .' and he spitefully but observantly described Mariella for *Der Spiegel* :

'Lauda's girl friend lives, outwardly at any rate, with the same troupe of technicians. But as she, unlike him, cannot use a machine but is turned in on herself, every bit of her behaviour is only a rehearsal of the real thing. People passing the pits see them sitting there perfectly motionless with their stop-watches taking the lap times, these wives or friends of the drivers, ridiculous and sad; ridiculous in that they know they are quite useless and therefore they cling to the little technical object, the stop-watch – sad, because silent and taciturn they have to suffer and endure.

Art student Mariella was not offended, she said at the time : 'For many people it's good that somebody should tear into the trashy conception of motor racing in such a brutal way. It is quite possible to see us in the way Handke did – with one eye, which looks only on the dark side.' The description of her Niki and of herself she had hoped might have been 'a little more subtle', and in this respect only the last sentence gave her something ('Some find it better to look out of the window – and, in the long run, more dangerous.')

Lauda himself only regretted the loss of time ('why did I explain things to him for three hours, when he was only thinking about the sexual act next door?') – and gave as good as he got. (Handke on Lauda : 'with a rather loud and, like a deaf person, slightly squeaky voice . . .'; Lauda on Handke : 'He doesn't speak normally, he whispers in one's ear.') And he drew the consequences of his short acquaintanceship with Peter Handke : 'Next time somebody comes and says "I know absolutely nothing about motor racing and can't even drive a car and I want to write about you", I shall reply : Fine, write, but don't ask me anything.'

He soon forgot this resolution, as the (not really comparable) example of Knef, two years later, proved.

*

The attempt to explain the motivation of motor racing built up the most audacious ideas based on Freud. The English psychologist Peter Fuller wrote a book lately, in which the psychoanalysis of motor racing gets a long chapter. Part of it rests on the assumption that there was a 'heroic' time in racing sport, about when Alberto Ascari was killed in 1955. On the grounds of a number of signs to which the superstitious Ascari gave certain meanings, Ascari is supposed to have known that he would die on that day. From this it was deduced that he sought death, and found it. The death-wish according to Fuller showed itself in that Ascari refused to wear his crash helmet, and that this was because his compulsive ego-defences broke down and he was overcome by his repressed instincts, including his libidinal castration-wish. The whole circumstances of his death are so overloaded with mysticism and superstition that it is impossible to relate them to modern times. But the idea that Ascari was on that day psychically disposed to have an accident, makes one pause. Involuntarily, whether one wishes to or not, this hypothesis makes one think of the situation before Lauda's Nürburgring accident. However much reason tells you that it is highly probable that a material defect was to blame, it is still a fact that in the days before the race Lauda thought a lot about the possibility of an accident. There are many witnesses to this, mostly journalists, who vouch for it. In one case a Lauda telephone conversation can still be heard because it was recorded for the Austrian journalist Dieter Stappert. It took place on the evening of 25th July 1976, that is to say one week before the accident.

LAUDA : . . . and now Nürburgring, two days' testing, tomorrow and the day after. There's nothing new, except gear-box problems. I quite dread the weekend, so boring, the important thing is to get through it alive, in my opinion, I don't know what the others think but that's what I think.

STAPPERT : Are there reserves for the Ring – not to go flat out – or once there must you go flat out ?

* Fuller, Peter : *Die Champions* : Psychoanalyse des Spitzen Sportlers, S. Fischer Verlag, Frankfurt.

LAUDA : That's it, you must, otherwise there's no point, and I know that now. I must but I don't want to. . . . If the crowd hisses when I appear I don't give a damn, let them hiss, I don't care, let the idiots hiss, and if nothing happens this weekend it will be a miracle, I can tell you that. And then on Monday we shall all say thank God, all of us. But the only people who understand this are those who've driven there. What other people say doesn't count. . . . Just take what happened a little while ago, the last accident, that was swinish. The death of Herr Rätz or whatever he was called wasn't thought important. But just imagine what would have happened if Fittipaldi had got burnt, if you see what I mean. It's madness, they take no notice of the other poor devil. If you hadn't written about it nobody would have, and that's murder. After the accident the race should have been stopped. As for the Ring – thank you very much, goodbye, I've had enough.

That he had a presentiment of the accident is nevertheless denied by Lauda. He says he was convinced of the stupidity of driving at Nürburgring, and that was why he spoke about it. He had thought of the possibility that a driver, *any* driver, might catch it there. When he is asked whether there is some truth in Fuller's thesis of his having felt it coming, he says : No, it was a race like any other.

This standpoint of Lauda's can be interpreted in two ways : (a) he considers his interior life too intimate to wish to speak about it, and chooses the easiest way out, (b) it is exactly as he says, which would only prove how easy it is for a learned man to build a whole theory on something which is as cogent as it is incorrect. For doubtless a parallel can be drawn between what Lauda said just before the race and the Ascari case, if somebody wishes to draw it.

*

In view of its claim of fundamental insight it is worth citing the quintessence of Peter Fuller's opinion about the motivation of motor racing. The English psychoanalyst considers that motor racing is compulsive. He asserts that its deeper causes lie in ambivalent impulses, which mostly stem from castration complex and rebellion against the father, and that motor racing is only justified and accepted because all the emphasis is laid on the technical side of it.

Lauda comments : 'I hope he understands what he's getting at. I don't.'

Lauda has no patience with Fuller's equation racing car – phallus, about which he writes pages (the pouring champagne over the winner is according to him ejaculation.) Lauda : 'Anyone can make comparisons if it amuses him. I have never bothered about such ideas, nor ever had the slightest feeling that my sort of racing driving has any connection at all with sex symbolism.'

Looking further into Fuller's book we came across two passages with which Lauda could more or less agree. The first expresses Fuller's opinion that the greatest need of the racing driver to dominate every aspect of his personality can be nothing else but resistance to powerful impulses which urge towards expression. He goes on to say that although the impulsive attraction, as psychologists demonstrate, is disguised and alien, it is not entirely hidden. Lauda had nothing to say against that; he knows his own impulsiveness, which he represses with the 'succession of technicalities' observed by Handke, giving rise to the computer image of him which the public gets.

Outside racing, and away from public view, he gives his impulsiveness free rein.

One bit of the Fuller book tickled me. It was about the results of an investigation that two Californian scientists carried out on two hundred American racing drivers. Lauda said straightaway: 'Two hundred American racing drivers, there just aren't as many as that.' Naturally there are a few thousand if you don't need any qualification, and no questions asked about the ability of those investigated. In any case the learned men came to the conclusion that the racing driver is a remarkably aggressive individual with a strong need to dominate; that he expresses his hostility verbally, holds his point of view energetically, assails any contrary opinion, and that his need to feel guilt, reproach himself and punish himself, is unusually small.

And how does Lauda see himself when he looks at the Californian picture? He says: 'The racing driver must be aggressive, otherwise you just don't drive fast. He must also want to dominate, otherwise you couldn't spend so much energy in the desire to be better than the others, to want to dominate them. Verbal hostility, well, yes, you could express it like that. Whether my need to feel guilty is unusually weak I don't know. I believe it's only important for people who make lots of mistakes. I give all my energy to not making mistakes – and I shouldn't be very successful if I continually felt guilty.'

3. Debunking

The New Vocabulary: Knights are out, Sacrifice is out,
Heroes are out

When Nuvolari won the Targo Florio in 1932, the poet
Gabriele d'Annunzio sent him this telegram :

Remember that when we parted I only laughed on one
side of my face, and I charged you to win the Sicilian race.
You have not forgotten the pact we made in the mourning
chamber. When we said farewell we were both certain of
victory, and so, never parted from comrades, it was even
more wonderful. Today your unbelievable achievement
makes you legendary. In the country called brilliant by the
great Imperator, I am with you and your people this evening.
I embrace you.

The sultry, heroic atmosphere which surrounded Nuvolari was
one extreme : ideological and mystical ideas overlay motor
racing, with every driver an angel of death. Today not only
Lauda but almost all racing drivers go to the other extreme,
with no trimmings on their de-mystified professionalism.
Lauda's attitude to his job :

is typical in its refusal of all ideology, in its austerity.

contains not the smallest interest in any idea of following
some tradition.

has no place for the heroic dimension.

Lauda says : 'I have never had a model', and appears to attach value to the fact of never having had a model. He says : 'I am myself'; he couldn't drive like Jim Clark, or think like Graham Hill, or look like Jochen Rindt – and nobody else could be like Niki Lauda. When at the age of fifteen in an old Volkswagen he jumped over ramps in his father's park, he didn't feel like Clark or Surtees but like Niki Lauda. That seems to point to the fact that he never lived in a dream world. Whatever you may call this unemotional attitude, it works in both directions. He did not want to *have* a model, and now he doesn't want to *be* one. He hasn't thought it over much, he only knows that it is so, that he doesn't feel called upon to serve as an example to youth. He naturally feels an obligation to the conventions, and as a public figure not to go off the rails, but that has nothing to do with any idea of mission. He gives, unconsciously and unintentionally, an example of the debunking of ideology in his sport.

Higher values, idealism, national fame : such abstract values are no longer accepted by the world's best performers. In the first twenty years of commercial sport they were often invoked, but now, gradually, they are left out of it. Naturally we still need 'higher values', but they are not to be found in sport. It is not idealism which urges on the 9.9 sprinter, the 8 metre jumper, the 50 second swimmer, the boxer or the racing driver. That the achievements of the specialists in common with the ideal of physical fitness are lumped together in the idea of 'sport' is simply to be seen from the technical side. All the same you still get false motives shoved onto people – 'fights for Austria' – you can't make it too clear that this doesn't happen. Lauda is more consistent than many of his colleagues; he makes it clear that he has nothing to do with idealism, he is simply *committed,* and draws from his commitment the way he strives towards his goal, free, neutral and unpolitical. As an 'example to youth' he is thus no more 'constructive' than most other top performers in sport, business, artists, politicians, public figures pure and simple. Any talk of higher values in his profession he regards as phoney and unnecessary.

Richard von Frankenberg, Germany's leading motor-sport writer in the fifties and sixties, describes in his biography of Count von Trips the following scene at the Mille Miglia in 1957, when Trips on the last stage caught up with Taruffi (both in Ferraris) :

'When Trips saw the other red car in front of him it was a great stimulus for him. After two rather slow corners he was lying directly behind Taruffi, and wanted to pass him. Then Taruffi pointed to the back axle, gesticulated, showed four fingers. Trips drove for a few seconds alongside Taruffi, who pointed forward and then put his hands together in an attitude of prayer. It was clear to our Wolfgang Trips what Taruffi wanted to say : "I can only go in fourth gear, there's something wrong with the back axle, let me go on, it is my last, my great chance just once to win this Mille Miglia." And in the next quick corner, which was done in fourth gear, Taruffi was especially fast, to show Trips he was in full control of the car and knew every metre of the route, but that he could no longer go flat out.

From then on Trips, although he could easily have overtaken Taruffi, stayed behind the old master . . . It was a gesture that Ferrari never forgot, a gesture, above all for Enzo Ferrari, that left a deep and enduring impression.'

This describes something that happened twenty years ago, but it reads like a story from the olden days. Apart from the fact that these drivers in short-sleeved shirts, with no seat belts, sat in their giant cars and drove through unprotected crowds of spectators, how unbelievably remote is the possibility

of such an attitude in the practice of motor-sport nowadays!
Trips compared motor-sport with the knights' tournaments of
the Middle Ages: 'For our sporting fight, such as in the old
days the knights fought, we use technical means . . . It is
traditional to put yourself to the test, and we, born into this
technical age, we have found a technical means, the motor
car.'

It goes without saying that neither Lauda nor any of his
professional colleagues see a grain of knightly tournaments in
motor-sport. On the other hand a man like Enzo Ferrari
probably finds it hard to think of motor-sport in purely
technical terms without emotional overtones.

That in the present-day Ferrari Team opinion on these
matters is confused, and that decison making is more tortuous
than it is with the English technical people, is explained by
this attitude. But it is too much to ask of any racing driver
that he should share these elevated feelings at Ferrari's.

Lauda does not feel linked with motor-sport tradition in
the very slightest, he doesn't classify himself in the stream of
historical names and events, he has no interest in 'ancestors'
or in learning more about former champions, or in looking for
resemblances. The nearest he comes to this is a certain
curiosity about Jim Clark, sometimes he asks the older
journalists: 'What was he really like?' because he never knew
him, and he has the feeling that Clark too, in comparison with
the other World Champions, was a bit different. He also said
he was moved when he saw pictures of Jochen Rindt – 'he
had a good head, he looks like a somebody, a personality' – but
that is all quite by the way. He doesn't *admire,* or *look up to*
any of them. He hasn't got the feeling that former World
Champions are in any way connected with him, or that he is
part of any tradition for the past or the future.

The heroic dimension is no longer a component of motor

racing. That is basically the logical consequence of the way the drivers see it, only the public is up to a point puzzled by somebody who thinks things out, counts the risks and at such and such a percentage of risk is not prepared to sacrifice himself. (Trips rated the willingness of self-sacrifice among the virtues of a racing driver, and part of the public sees it in the same way. Expressed by a psychoanalyst – Fuller : The popular image of the racing driver remains, because the fans . . . identify themselves also with the part of the driver which risks the loss of mastery. Stewart was set aside because with his style of driving and his insistence on safety this aspect of him practically disappeared).

Lauda will have nothing to do with talk of bravery or courage; he says he must first get a definition; what is courage? A possible answer was given by the French poet Jules Renard when he wrote : 'You do not have courage, but moments of courage . . . there are not happy and unhappy people, only happy and unhappy moments in time.'

Therefore courage is not a theme for Lauda and men like him, they find this kind of vocabulary trashy and unnecessary. 'Nobody can help me when I have to go out and know I must drive a chaotic lap and drive like a madman, in order to get pole position.'

4. Embracing the Masses

Does the love of the masses generate enough power to enable the masses to be loved? Public Relations in practice

'With the first shilling you take from the public you throw away the right to complain about public criticism.'

STIRLING MOSS.

Lauda became enormously better known through his accident. To be half burnt and make a comeback six weeks later even impressed the Americans, who generally haven't much use for Formula I sport. By the end of 1977 Lauda was probably, next to Muhammed Ali, the best known sportsman world-wide, with a built-in potential market value of which he only used a fraction. Not exactly because he despised money, but because he needs so much strength for his sport, so much time to recover his strength, that business is secondary. He only takes what comes easily.

His popularity in central Europe had already in 1975 reached and passed what was desirable.

LAUDA : 'As long as you are a little nobody, you are naturally pleased when for the first time you hear "Look, aren't you Lauda?" and it gets better and better, you are given privileges, and you use them and enjoy them, until at some moment you get to the point where it is too much, you don't enjoy it any more.'

But of course he can't opt out now, he knows he's got to live with it, and he manages very well, much better than some

144

less well-known racing drivers. Apart from the basic work – testing, racing – and his private life, everything he does is of necessity geared to publicity. This contact with the public has six aspects: the Media – the sponsors – action for giving out news – racing-car shows – direct contact with the fans – fan-mail.

His relationship with journalists is one of Lauda's most brilliant successes. He is first class at judging the importance of the media, in distinguishing between professional and un-professional journalists, in what show to put on for the latter, in the economy of time, in keeping quiet about anything 'unsuitable' (for himself or for his firm) in the difference between truth and the 'political' truth of the moment. That is for example the difference between what is published in this book and the interviews he gave at the time, to the daily and the specialist press – when it was quite impossible for him to say 'everything'. It would have cost him his job. At that time he only told one specialist writer, the Austrian Dieter Stappert whom he absolutely trusted, 'everything'. Stappert knew without asking what was meant for publication – often only a tenth of the recorded telephone conversation.

Lauda always tries to compress all the interviews together at the training stage before the race, for reasons of economy, because all the reporters are there and they know there's not much time and the procedure must be condensed. With the real specialists who are worth something and who only ask necessary and sensible questions (there are about a dozen of them, world-wide) everything runs smoothly and there are no problems, though also with them Niki is incredibly fussy and pedantic. The better he knows one of these journalists the harder he is on him if he detects (seen subjectively) a mistake in his newspaper article.

Except at press conferences or proper public relations exercises, Lauda answers with hectic speed whenever he talks to a journalist. He always says he's got no time, unless they look sharp, and so the questioner has no chance for round-about methods and Lauda snaps out his answers, which gives an impression of dynamism. This is an excellent technique, rather like rapid-reading: the condensed press interview. He uses the same technique with the few chosen journalists who have got his private telephone number (though apparently the circle widens, so that every few months the number has to be changed.)

Because of his enormous popularity in Austria, the motor-sport writers in the Vienna daily papers cannot afford to let him alone for a few days, they must check up on him almost daily, and at critical times more than once a day. Critical times are when change is in the air (giving notice to Ferrari, the contract with Brabham) or when it is uncertain whether he will race (after accidents with cars and tractors), when there are rumours of marriage, or of a baby on the way. Those journalists who can get hold of him naturally fall into the role of court reporters. Even a terribly critical and sceptical journalist like Helmut Zwickl (*Kurier*) can't allow himself to be sceptical when it comes to Lauda, because Niki would never again allow him in the front row. (Zwickl used to be a Lauda opponent, and wagered that Niki would never get a bank loan; afterwards he had to serve in the ranks before Lauda took him into the inner circle of those he trusted.)

Pestering sometimes pays. A woman reporter from *Paris Match* wanted an interview; Niki didn't want it. He had a feeling that this lady would probably ask him silly questions, and then he was annoyed that she had used his private telephone. In any case he refused time after time, and the reporter always rang up again.

Niki: 'It got so on my nerves that I exploded.'

The explosion resulted in Niki saying, 'Tomorrow at ten, ten punctually, I'll give you an hour. Adieu.'

Despite the routine in his relations with journalists Lauda is flexible and can change in a second to 'specialist treatment'. When *Newsweek* asked him for interviews for a cover-story, Lauda was in the midst of the decisive time of preparation for giving notice at Ferrari's. During such times he tries in every way to put everything aside and concentrate on the only thing that matters. However, for *Newsweek* he decided he would play, which he did as requested, naturally giving them a few 'political' truths, for he was still at Ferrari's. It didn't worry him that *Newsweek* sent three or four reporters, he even answered a few (for him) 'silly' questions, the sort that usually finished a reporter as far as he went. (One of the reporters came up with the old Ferrari complaint that Lauda shouldn't have started to drive again so soon after his accident. Such themes, once discussed and dealt with and 'ended' are a terrific turn-off for Lauda.)

Newsweek got this special treatment because Lauda reckoned to reach a world-wide audience who in the ordinary way knew nothing about motor racing – and for his future profession in the aeroplane business Lauda wanted a good image in the international business world. It speaks for Niki as a tactician and as a person that the *Newsweek* story was highly advantageous to him, apart from two mistakes for which he was to blame : he used the words 'pompous bastard' about his grandfather, and called the Italians 'a goddam fanatical nation' . . . both were quite enough to make people think again about his image as a 'computer'. Only an impulsive man would speak in such a way, somebody who doesn't weigh his words. He didn't really mean it, about his rich grandfather. Although he hadn't very much time for him, the words quoted were only the result of carelessness, and the same goes for what he said about the Italians. He used an expression carelessly and any of us might thoughtlessly do the same.

Taken as a whole the eight-page *Newsweek* story was relatively straightforward decent reporting on the theme of Lauda and motor racing; it was not particularly profound but there were no important mistakes. It was an immense public relations success for Lauda.

The same thing happened when, a few weeks later, *Der Spiegel* wanted to do a cover-story. Lauda had the strain of the race at Monza immediately after he had given in his notice, nevertheless he made room for the *Spiegel* people in his head and his heart. Lauda's satellites say that they can never remember him so patient and willing during a photography session as he was in the middle of the training stage at Monza when a *Spiegel* girl photographer was shooting the cover picture. Lauda always works remarkably well with women, so long as they are fairly attractive and know what they are doing. In any case the whole thing was well worth while. Under the title: 'Not God, but like a god' a very favourable *Spiegel* story appeared, really remarkable for a magazine which hitherto had treated motor racing in a blasé and intellectually arrogant way. The *Spiegel* reporters did not make the same mistake as some others in their trade; they hinted at a different, gambling, impulsive Lauda, who was anything but a computer.

Lauda gets angry when the expert journalists give what he considers a misrepresentation of facts, but he doesn't mind in the slightest what the ordinary newspapers and magazines write about him. He even sometimes helps them, and puts his name to it, if they pay enough. He divides the media into two groups: the same inaccuracy which in *Das Bild* would slightly annoy him would make him furious in a 'normal' paper. And fastidious and reserved as he is about publicity touching his private life, nevertheless *Quick* can write his love-stories; but only by paying terrific sums in compensation. He just grinned when *Bunte* on the front page whetted the reader's appetite with : 'How Niki and Ali became friends'. Niki had seen Muhammed Ali for a quarter of an hour in New York and thought him the bottom, but that would hardly do as the story to go with the world-exclusive picture of Lauda and Ali (on Ali's bed.)

Lauda was disgusted by the way *Das Bild* reported his Nürburgring accident week by week. All the same, he visited the *Bild* editors a year later, and posed with them as their guest. Why, Niki?

LAUDA : 'I don't identfy the man who rings me up forty-five times to ask me to visit the editors a hundred per cent with his paper. When I have thought of forty-five excuses and can't think of a forty-sixth, the whole thing has become such a bore that I want to get it over with quickly. And I know it's good for the reporter Ramsauer if he manages to get me to Hamburg. Ramsauer himself isn't responsible for the *Bild* headlines, he tries to be objective, and that makes his job especially difficult. It's a non-stop struggle for him, he's always under pressure. For instance in the days before the race in Brazil in 1977 he came to me and said : "I've got a message from the paper, that your wife is expecting a baby." No, I say, my wife isn't expecting a baby.

Then he got quite serious and worried and said : "Please, are you quite sure? Because if I write that your wife isn't expecting a baby, but in fact she really is, I shall be sacked on the spot."

Then I say : Look out, Herr Ramsauer, your paper gets on my nerves, I tell you officially that *so far as I know my wife isn't expecting a baby,* does that satisfy you? Then of course he has to say yes.

'Early next day he's there again, embarrassed : "Herr Lauda, I've got an enormous request. Could you possibly say what you told me yesterday on my recording machine, so that I can play it over on the telephone to the editor in Hamburg?

Because he doesn't believe me." Then I get really angry and I shout into the thing: *"I'm not having a baby. That's a statement by Niki Lauda in the Hilton Hotel at Sao Paulo and now you can go to hell."* You can imagine how Ramsauer has to fight at *Bild*. And when I make the effort and fly to Hamburg for coffee with these people, I only do it for him, because I feel sorry for him. But naturally only when he goes on and on until I can't bear it.'

The popular press trampled around on his private life and published things that were pure invention, but all the same they were favourable to Niki. He is the type that what might be called the Soraya media, the gossip columnists, like best; which explains his unconcern about all the rubbish they write.

As far as the direction of his international image goes, Niki is as helpless as any other star. There is nothing he can do when some left-wing English journalist feels left out of things and writes in his paper, the charming little mouse has turned into a sewer rat. The natural fury which seizes him is amusing to watch, and in the language of his image you could say: The computer is boiling. This helpless rage is part of the hardening process which all famous people have to go through.

Much more simple and much more profitable than the journalists are the sponsors. All they cost is time, before the contract is signed. There's no harm in the people who want their advertisements on overalls or crash helmet, like Parmalat, Marlboro, Raiffeisen, Römerquelle, all they want is value for money. Even wearing Matra pullovers isn't too difficult for the champion. Then there are Goodyear, *Autorevue;* Lauda sun glasses for the eyes, Lauda jeans for the behind, no problem. Fiat, and now Alfa-Romeo, consider it an honour to have one of their cars in Lauda's garage, next to the 12 cylinder Jaguar given by Leyland. Also the driving of Honda and KTM is free and only linked with minimal signs of gratitude. In general the permanent business contracts are the most advantageous, and also take least time.

Lauda demands a prohibitive price for personal appearances. An hour of writing autographs costs as much as the month's salary of a business director. It must be so, says Lauda, because it takes so much out of him; the journey, the crowds, having to look friendly, the writing in the hectic press of people. If he's not offered enough he refuses to do it: 'I'd rather rest. As there are not many firms which can pay so much, I don't have many autographing sessions.' And again: 'I can only command big money as long as I am on top. Nobody will want me if I lose, or give up.' This is known as free market economy, he may be calculating, but then so is the 'market'. The only thing that counts is success. So why should he give special prices? Everyone can follow Lauda's reasoning here.

The man in the street finds it harder to understand that it doesn't give Lauda a tremendous kick to be spoken to by him, to have a nice chat with him. After all, we know each other, I've known you so long, I always watch you on the telly, I always hold my thumbs for you. Lauda is enough of a professional only to push such people out of the way when the pressure is too great and the pain-threshold has been reached. Otherwise he is nicer and more welcoming than might be imagined. Which of us would care to live with what happens to him all the time; when he stops at a red light somebody presses a bit of paper on the window of the car: 'Listen I haven't got a pen, have you got one?' and Niki lets down the window and gets his ball-point pen and writes on the scrap of paper. He used to have a lovely signature, he used to put LAUDA with a long stroke on the L which began the N for Niki, in block letters. Such autographs he writes no longer. If you really possess one of these rarities I would only swop it with an Elvis Presley.

On the race course and at racing-car shows the writing of autographs is part of the work of a World Champion – he is realist enough to know this. He just does it as quickly as he can, in and out. Autographs forced out of him in the stadium deserve a punch.

That he doesn't go into crowds now unless it's necessary anyone can understand who has spent a couple of hours in the tail of the comet. Avoiding people sometimes entails grotesque detours, for example, he was in the Vienna TV studio on a Monday evening and had to be early on Tuesday at Zeltweg, 250 km south of Vienna, and used his private jet for that. But rather than spend the night at an hotel in Vienna he flew all the way back to Salzburg (300 km west) and then early next day to Zeltweg. The reason : to stay the night in Vienna got on his nerves. He didn't want to be stared at in the Intercontinental, he hates the moment when he's recognized at the reception desk. When he flies home and then early next day flies again he only sees the flying personnel, and they are absolutely okay, and so he can sleep in his incomparable bed at home, at the edge of the forest. Nobody has taken more trouble to get home in all circumstances, and this is the great advantage of a private jet. To have a jet to fly *away* with has become old-fashioned.

LAUDA : 'Public figure, okay. All the same I can choose whether to let myself be gaped at or not. A bit of flying around is worth it, to get peace and sleep at home. I come home and I'm myself; in the hotel I wake early and I'm always Lauda.'

On the race-course Lauda does what he can to satisfy the fans. If they interrupt when he's talking to somebody, which often happens, they get a growl of *'Later';* and sometimes, when it's not *his day* he can seem so gloomy and aggressive that his satellites automatically shelter him from people. And then of course his departure; if somebody gets in his way or holds him up he isn't treated in a friendly way. He is always fixed on his goal, no question.

'My darling most beloved Niki! You don't know me, but I know you terribly well . . .' Fan mail. The Champion has become an Idol. Letters (mostly to the offices of the Vienna *Autorevue,* also through Ferrari's and to his Salzburg address) amount to about 2,500 a month. Supposing he were to deal with them all he would have to have a special office, quickly read the text, dictate a short answer and sign his autograph, which would take about 90 seconds. This would mean 60 hours work a month. So he answers at random a couple of times a month and signs until his hand begins to hurt (rather soon) and that's it, for the post. It is all he can do.

You can catalogue Niki Lauda's fan mail, but no picture of the *average fan* emerges. The reasons for writing are so far apart that they have no common denominator. The biggest group (60%) remain faceless; on the letters or cards just a simple request for an autograph with no embellishments. The remainder of the letters can be divided into age groups.

Children Almost the only motive is to become racing drivers.

Dear Herr Lauda :
I should like to congratulate you heartily on your victory, over Scheckter, at Kyalami. Unfortunately Tom Pryce died there. You drove a terrific race. I followed it on television. Jean Pierre Jarier is the half uncle of my friend E.S. We are both very interested in motor racing. Our dream is to become racing drivers. We were at school four years toegther. Now he's at high-school and I'm at middle school. I am prefect of my class. I was born on 10th February 1966, son of a driving teacher. I was top of the 4th form. I collect pictures of racing sport and I've got about 1,300 pictures, 400 are of you. Erwin and I can already drive a little. My speed record is about 70

km/h. Erwin's is about 40 km/h. Could you please send me a letter with your autograph? I enclose the stamps for your reply. I weigh 31 kilos, am 140 cm tall, I take Number 35 size shoes and I've got a little dog. I have never broken a bone and went to Judo for a year. A photo of me is at the end of this letter. Could you come and visit me? Could you please send me your Salzburg telephone number? I have been learning the jazz trumpet for about two years. I follow all the races that are given on television. I consider it's a good achievement (1975 first in world championship, 1976 second, 1977?) I hope you will be World Champion in 1977. Could you please describe the race at Nürburgring from the start until your accident? I hope this year it will go well again. Could you help me to become a racing driver?

Your faithful fan : H. E. P. Passail.

P.S. Could you please send me the wiring diagram of your Ferrari (Formula I).

Next come young people, who use the same fan expressions as they do for pop stars or actors. Three quarters of these letter writers address their hero with the familiar *Du* – which is logical, for they feel they know him well enough. There are just about as many girls as boys. They make small requests, ask many questions, but mostly just want to *chat*. They give advice of course, and show family feeling; most of them send best greetings to Marlene.

The way the young girl who wrote the next letter idolizes Niki, is the nearest thing to a 'love letter'. Real declarations of love from women are very rare. Perhaps the reason is that Niki Lauda's erotic radiation to the public is quite weak, and this is Niki's own opinion : 'Well, it's normal that a married man doesn't get proposals, so they never get such ideas.' And what was it like before you married? 'I don't know, I've never read my fan mail.'

My darling darling beloved Niki!

You don't know me but I know you especially well. I am a 14 year old fan of yours and I think you're marvellous. I am German but I live in Rome. I saw your race at the beginning of 1975 on television from Monte Carlo, the Grand Prix when you beat the old World Champion Emerson Fittipaldi. I found it so thrilling and exciting, and since then I follow all the races you are in. I've got a Swiss friend who has met James Hunt, Emerson Fittipaldi and Jackie Stewart. Also poor Tom Pryce, my second favourite driver, next to you. Unluckily I lost him at Kyalami. . . .

You are and always will be my one and only Formula I star. But since your terrible accident at Nürburgring I am so frightened for you. I think you are the bravest Formula I driver I have ever known. On my writing table there's a heart-shaped photo of you. Your books *Ferrari Mondiale* of 1975, *10 e la corsa,* the World Champion 1975 Ferrari 312 B3 model, in which I've put a cut-out photo of you, and lots more photographs of you, I keep carefully. My whole room is papered with posters of you and your wonderful Ferrari.

I like you so much, but may I ask you a question. I read in the paper of 30th August that you want to leave your dear Ferrari, and next year probably drive a Brabham Alfa. But why? Why are you leaving the best Formula I car of recent times? I don't say that because Ferrari is Italian, but for technical reasons. I would like to give you a bit of advice : please stay in the Maranello team, or you will certainly regret it.

Now I wish you my most beloved to be the marvellous winner of the 1977 world championship, and lots of happiness, great successes and a happy future,

Your fan from Rome, Sabrina.

P.S. Be careful when you go in your private plane. Think of

(continued on page 175)

Comments on the following color picture series

The theme of the color picture series is not the person of Niki Lauda, but the world of his professional life, Grand Prix racing in general.

Among the world's best motor sport photographers we chose the Swiss photographer, Carl Imber, who took all of the pictures on the sixteen succeeding pages. Imber also wrote the following explanations which enable the reader to compare the photographer's reflections and the final result — the published picture.

159 On every racing day there is the same main question: From which approach should I take a picture of the start today? On the one hand, I would prefer to have a different angle every time, but on the other hand, the customers prefer a start as "custom in trade" rather than a shot from the back or an exaggerated zoom exposure. In Hockenheim the privileged seats for photographers are often in a more disadvantageous place than the regular spectators' grandstands. In order to take this photograph I was standing on a beer case behind the last row of the grandstand. The camera with 300 mm telelens and motordrive preserved the ramming against Regazzoni and his retirement. The people at the pitstops give the impression of ants, although they are not as organized.

160 Of all types of sport, it is in motor racing where you can take pictures of the most beautiful and interesting women. James Hunt, Carlos Reutemann and John Watson certainly have no objections.

161 Once again, the classical, simple and incapricious picture of a start (above); this time in Zandvoort. The position of the camera is obvious: above the Tarzan bend. Below, duel in the Tarzan bend: Peterson and Jarrier are almost leveling. I have to consider three factors: Which shutter speed will provide the prettiest blurred background? Should I include the red fire extinguisher in the foreground in the composition of the picture? In addition, I have to watch if a dramatic scene develops out of this situation. I have to follow with the camera in order to be ready in case of a crash at the exit of the bend. If an editor reads about a collision on such and such lap, he will ask me: Where is the picture?

162 Another contribution to the subject of 'ladies'; this time they surround Niki Lauda, Hans Stuck and Jacques Laffite. Below right, on the pier of Monaco is Nina Rindt.

163 The starting laps at Monaco (above, with Scheckter in front) and Jarama (we recognize Andretti, Laffite, Reutemann, Scheckter, Hunt and Watson. In the second group Regazzoni leads in front of Mass and Depailler). Monaco is — regardless of all precautions — the most dangerous place for racing photographers.

164 Nice frame for Peterson and Scheckter, Rupert Keegan, Emerson Fittipaldi and Patrick Depailler.

165 Niki Lauda in Jarama. This is a place I go to see every year. I try to detach the Ferrari from its surroundings with a 500 mm SLR telelens and preserve the dynamics of the car, to freeze the speed so to speak.

166 Technology and mechanics, colors, shapes and people — during two practice sessions in the drivers' camp.

167 Mario Andretti. The attempt to give an interpretation of cornering from a photographic point of view: black, gold and speed. The picture is taken at the 'Bahnhofskurve' in Monaco; nowhere else in the Grand Prix circus can you get that close to the cars. From a distance of two meters and an elevated position, I followed with a slow shutter speed (1/15 sec) and simultaneously zoomed from wide angle to tele-range (from 35 mm to 90 mm).

168 Final preparations of Lauda's Ferrari. Below, Lauda and Patrick Depailler during the last seconds before the start. On the Tyrrell you can see the very small window which enables the driver to check the condition of the front tires.

169 John Watson coming out of the bend. The yacht harbor of Monaco makes a terrific scene. This track is a comforting contrast to the modern racing tracks where the surroundings cannot be included in the picture, as they consist only of boards and wire fences.

170 What comes with a race — i.e. show and security guard (typical for the Argentine Grand Prix). Siesta: Depailler. Conversation: Rega-Fitti. We, the 'Wunderkinder' (the prodigal children): Lauda-Cecotto. Waiting: Hunt, Teddy Mayer and—having day dreams—a guest, Barry Sheene.

171 When bad light conditions prevail, the photographer has to concentrate on the right choice of light-sensitive lenses and correct shutter speeds. The emotional reactions show only with the first examination of the developed picture: Heavens, what effort it must take to drive in such conditions!

172 This exposure with the 400 mm lens produces a picture that the spectators will never be able to see at the track. The strong telelens changes the perspective in such a way that it does not correspond to reality. In actuality, the Lotus and the Tyrrell are not that close together, but the telelens dramatizes the situation, thus reducing the disadvantages of a motionless picture and giving, as a final result, the right impression.

173 Above, Niki Lauda framed in gold. With the help of the completely blurred foreground resulting from the flowers of Monaco, it is possible to manipulate the beauty of the racing car, the beauty of the technology as such, and the

photographer is able to provoke emotions. Below, Scheckter tailgates Stuck. This exposure has also deliberately been taken with the long telelens to emphasize the impression of fighting. At a boring track, like Jarama, you have no other choice than to concentrate with all possible tricks on the cars— otherwise there is nothing other than fences and boards. You can't even find blades of grass that could possibly be included in the picture as a blurred foreground.

174 Grand Prix—a sport for the people, with an incredible number of spectators and all that goes with mass display such as hysteria, craziness and glaringness of advertising. Sometime or another, everyone will be in a situation where they will close their eyes and hold their ears for a brief moment, and a picture similar to the one below will flash through their brains.

(continued from page 155)

poor Carlos Pace, Graham Hill and Tony Brise, who have all been killed recently.

Live happily with your Marlene, and be happy with your Ferrari.

Once again I wish you all the best.

There is also another kind of fan mail from young people with enclosures and little presents, usually drawings or poems, or home-made model cars.

A poem for Austria's fabulous, beloved and intelligent Formula I motor racing driver Niki Lauda, who has shown exemplary courage, ambition, endurance and tremendous will-power. (In my opinion the best racing driver of all time.)

Dedicated by M. W. Graz.

Many thought you were already dead, Niki Lauda, marvellous Formula I driver. But the unbelievable happened. Niki recovered from all his woes. Although some wrote him off, he remained the greatest driver. His success is his own, with his great ability he nevertheless did not get it easily, he had many struggles until he rose so far and climbed to the highest rung of the ladder. With strong will and effort, sweat often ran from his brow, Niki fought his way through. Everyone surely knows you do not get so far without talent. Although he was the favourite, and his successes the greatest hit. What his friends hoped for, Niki succeeded in doing, with his ambition and his will. Lauda is also clever, and that shows in his way with the car; the Ferrari managers saw to it that the car was constantly modified. After such a serious accident it takes great courage to win again : I wish for Niki the world championship title this year, I truly do. Hats off to such a man, whom one can look up to. I hope too that he will be happy, that everything will go right for him. Niki Lauda, Austria's greatest motor-racing idol.

Graz 25 August 1977

The average letter from a grown-up person to Niki Lauda relates interesting things from the sender's life, with useful tips. The most important part is the will to *communicate*.

Dear* Herr Lauda, dear Frau Lauda :
I have long had the desire to write you a few lines.
First I must congratulate you on your successes in the 1977 season, which is not quite over. I hope you will be World Champion '77.
I wish and hope that your accident is completely behind you, not least because of your driving ability, but also because of the strength you get from your dear wife at your side. As a fisherman I also know the problems which a great driver has, namely the unknown quantity, the machine. You will perhaps think that a madman is writing to you, but it's not quite the case; I have only given my whole sympathy to two drivers in my life, they are you and my dead friend Alberto Ascari from Italy. I see a real world champion before me.
People say you are a computer. I deny this, for a computer drives only in a straight line. You, and Ascari, are more to me than that.
Lately I spoke to one of your countrymen in Italy, as to whether people in Germany will hold it against you that you are so severe about the 'Ring'; I gave the answer, hardly anyone who knows the Ring blames Herr Lauda. I personally saw Onofri Marimon fly through the hedge and I know from driving round the Ring that anyone who does the times you do must have something done about it, and make the German public understand. So don't worry, nobody in Germany blames you. These lines were already overdue when you had your accident, and I hope they will give you some strength, even

* Note by translater. These letters begin *Sehr geehrter Herr Lauda,* i.e. 'honoured Herr Lauda' which is of course an unknown form of address in England and can only be translated by 'Dear'.

if you don't really need it. Unfortunately I only know you from your picture, I haven't even got your autograph, which I would be most grateful for. If ever it were possible I should love to drink a glass of wine with you. Until then I wish you and your dear wife all the best and good luck at Zandvoort.

If this letter is opened by a secretary, I should be most grateful if later on it could be shown to Herr Lauda.

Heinz S. Dortmund.

Great rarities are letters which come, not from fans but simply from people who have a point to make, and which from beginning to end are to be taken seriously. One of these letters is on page 98, it is about the interview that Lauda gave, and which the newspapers distorted, immediately after he had given notice at Ferrari's (the 'slack bosom' letter.)

Czechoslovakia : In the eastern block there seems to be an unbelievable hunger for everything to do with motor sport. About one sixth of all Lauda's fan mail comes from there.

Dear Niki,

For the last few years I have been your fanatical fan. Since in 1972 you raced at Brno in Czechoslovakia, I have been your fanatic. And now, in five years, you are the most popular F.I. driver. I am happy that I did not make a mistake about your art. I should very much like to have your photo with signature. And therefore I am writing to you. I did write to you two years ago, but perhaps I had the wrong address (in Vienna). Now I only know that you live at Salzburg. I think you will get the letter, because you are so well-known. Perhaps you could grant my request.

I was very pleased when in 1975 you won the world championship. But your damage at the Nürburgring, that was a nasty surprise. First we heard news that you were all right.

But after a week I found out that you suffered terrible injuries.

I admired your gesture in Japan, when you abandoned this dangerous Grand Prix. You only live once. How can Hunt get any joy from the title, that I don't understand. I believe this year you will win the world champion title and I wish you much luck for it.

I ask you once again, please send me a photo with your own signature on it. I thank you heartily. If I could ask one thing more, please send me a letter. Much success and more luck is what your fan from Czechoslovakia wishes you.

Zdenek Bezedek.

P.S. Please forgive my terrible German.

Insults : Abusive letters are rare, and they are usually anonymous, like this one (the writing points to an elderly person).

Hardly had you snatched the shovel from the grave-digger, according to the newspapers, than you started again, cold as ice, and drove as before; but they forgot one thing, James Hunt must have a defect in his car, otherwise you would never have come home as victor from South Africa. That you are as cold as ice the newspapers could have meant in another way, you didn't stop, you didn't help, for you the win was more important than a comrade of yours, Tom Pryce. You were saved, otherwise you would now be looking at the potatoes from underneath, you ice-cold man you. You had luck when a bit of Tom Pryce's car got under your car but nothing happened to you, if that had happened to someone else, something would certainly have gone wrong, but you have more luck than brains in your life, and you can thank your colleagues for that, that you are still alive. You think you are the greatest, but the day will come when you too will catch it, unfortunately the wrong one caught it and had to die, you were the one who should have caught it, so that there's

178

peace in the Lauda business. Your colleague Prüller seems to be married to you, one hears only Lauda, Lauda, nothing else, when he is reporter on television, it makes it uninteresting to watch when Prüller is reporting. Herr Prüller can stick you in his hat as a souvenir. Your wife said today you will be World Champion, but you must wait, there are still others around who will get the money and not Lauda. Perhaps your wife can buy you a wreath as victor, then you can be off as soon as possible. Your victories and so on don't interest many Austrians. For years Mariella Reininghaus was good enough, now no longer, but God will punish, you should have died, but the day will come, God's punishment is everywhere. Lastly, you have more luck than brains, and there is a motto 'Stupid people have good luck.'

We do not begrudge anyone the World Champion title, except you. (Anonymous).

A man for all ages : Older people also write to Lauda. Unlike the young fans, the letters are very different according to the sex of the writer. Elderly ladies write very charming letters, usually like this :

Dear Herr Lauda,

Although I am a woman of fifty I am a great and enthusiastic admirer of yours. I was delighted by your wins and was very worried about you when you were injured. My friends laugh at me, because my greatest wish is to have your picture with autograph. May I hope?

Many thanks and once again I wish you much success.

E. F. Zell/see.

The older *gentlemen* give very forceful advice, for example:

Dear Lauda,

The *Kronenzeitung* reports that you are going to try stunt-flying. Now, once already you have been saved from the flames, and now you want to go into new dangers. Keep your fingers out of it; if you become World Champion once again you will collect enough money to give up this sport. We have enough dead racing drivers, and the young women who have lost their husbands in this way are not to be envied. Rupert Hollans, Dirtl, Rindt, were all young men who would like to be alive, I have spoken with Rindt myself about the danger of this sport, and a few months later he was dead. Health is the greatest capital, money is necessary but not at the cost of health. I am 76 and have lived through many experiences, but I have never gone into danger unless it was absolutely necessary. Three years in Russia and always the luck to survive, more times than one can count, and now I am a pensioner and wouldn't change with a racing driver however much money and what goes with it he had carried off. I could tell you a lot, but I hope you will mind my words and give up soon.

For Zeltweg I wish you victory, so that you can become World Champion as soon as possible and then make an end of it.

F. K. Sieghartskirchen.

As already said, the communication is one sided. Long letters, full pages come in, thin autographed postcards go back. Apart from the technical impossibility of giving each individual correspondent 'full service', Niki couldn't give his audience what they give him. He simply cannot understand why they do it, the whole thing is foreign to his nature, and it perplexes him when he thinks about it. The most he can manage is to be kind, even when he can't understand : 'Oh well, if it gives him pleasure. . . .' On the same plane is his indifference to the demands of would-be racing drivers. The very fact that somebody should *ask* how to become a racing driver, or if he has to be helped along the way, means that in his eyes this man has no qualification at all. Self-assertion and a lonely struggle is not the *way* to motor sport but an essential ingredient of it. You cannot sever motor racing from its environment, or confine it to technical matters. Getting yourself a car is just as important as the driving of it. This is his professionalism : a career, whatever it may be, in sport, in a profession or in business, has the same rules everywhere.

5. Beside the Way

The private life of a public figure

Niki, you catch a frog in the stream. The frog says I give you three wishes if you let me go. What is your answer? After ten seconds consideration, Lauda says quickly: First I wish for a child, second I wish for my professional pilot's licence, properly endorsed according to Austrian requirements, third I wish for my own freight flying business, already established and functioning. 'But,' he added, 'those are my wishes *today*, tomorrow it may all look quite different.' So let us give the date: 26th October 1977.

Meanwhile the racing driver dominates the man. Even his private life is overshadowed by his standard vocabulary: physique, reserves, building up, pulling down, over the limit.

He distinguishes between two sorts of activity: Building up and pulling down. When the pulling down goes so far that the physique (that is his bodily, spiritual, nervous capacity) is attacked, then the situation is 'over the limit' and must – almost violently – be changed at once.

His life, both public and private, balances day in day out along this niveau line, as if it was on the surface of the water, now over, now under, and gets the necessary adjustment.

The upset of a night out with alcohol and too many cigarillos, (yes, really) naturally brings such a sharp dent in the line that the timing must be right. He calls it 'opening the safety-valve' because he says 'otherwise you would go mad'. He chooses the moment for opening the safety-valve with care, and looks forward to it with a certain grim anticipation.

The people round him must fall in with all this. His private life, and even his marriage, are completely integrated with his sport, and everyone is ready to fit in with him.

In his own words this state of affairs is clear; as Stirling Moss once said: 'My predilection for motor racing is an obsession which has destroyed my personal relationships.'

LAUDA: 'The word obsession sounds bad, too negative. I am not obsessed by sport, but I am good at it, I am *very* good at it. The word obsession perhaps describes it rightly, but it has a nasty undertone. Apart from that, I can very well imagine personal relationships being destroyed. With me it begins with the fact that I am never free. I'm always carrying a rucksack, for example the following: I know the races are going to be even more difficult and that next year I must give even more, I must intensify everything. But as this year I gave a hundred per cent, where am I going to get this increase? I have to concentrate my whole life in order to be able to manage this improvement. Even in the simplest ways, for example: On seventeen Sundays in the year I mustn't have a cold. If I get a cold a fortnight before a race that's fine, it will be over in time. If I catch cold one week before the race it's critical, and therefore I often have to behave like an overstrained opera singer. Not too warm, not too cold, no draughts and so forth.

'I can't be crazy when I want to be. If I go out in the evening and get back late, I can't sleep. On the whole I am anyway so stretched that I only do what's absolutely necessary. Whatever happens, the sport is always there and it overshadows everything. At this time it's naturally difficult for people who live with me to get along with me. You need a very special sort of wife. This business of a "special wife" was once dragged out of me and I've thought it over since and it's true. I was once with a girl in a nightclub and all the time people came asking me for autographs. Every few minutes somebody came to our table and disturbed us – as unfortunately always happens. The girl grumbled all the time, "It's mad when one's with you, there's not a moment's peace, I can't bear it" – and at the same time I noticed she was avid for the publicity. Then she said, "One couldn't marry a man like you", and I wanted my peace and quiet and said, "That's it then. Special men need special wives – and you don't belong there."

'If I had a wife who didn't accept the special circumstances of my profession and who didn't take me as I am, it would never work. It didn't work with Moss, nor with Jim Clark and it didn't work with me either. Motor racing has to come first, before one's wife.'

The rules of priorities in Lauda's home have grown into a very comfortable Austrian solution which is much easier and more normal than it sounds in theory. Marlene has many characteristics which are particularly helpful for living with an unusual man. She is cheerful, uncomplicated, not possessive and independent enough to be able to go her own way for hours, days or weeks.

Marlene's parents are an Austrian artist and a Spanish woman. The couple wandered around a good deal and their children were born in different places. The first was born in Spain, the second (Marlene) in Venezuela, the third and fourth in Chile. As well as the nationality of their place of birth the children were naturally Austrian citizens like their father. Marlene on her South American childhood : 'One day my father decided to be a farmer instead of a painter. He bought some land in Chile and began raising cattle. My first recollections are of animals, all sorts of animals, from the spider-catcher bird to the puma. We went to school in a boat and were taught to do everything for ourselves. A bad earthquake wrecked Valdivia, the town near us, and then my father wanted more than ever to live in the country. He was erratic and went from one project to another. Once he got a machine for extracting eucalyptus oil, then something went wrong and the whole thing rusted. Then he built cow-byres for 200 cows, at the end we had ten cows and a few hundred bats there. Bit by bit we lost all the cows, mostly they were stolen. The family just didn't know enough about farming.'

As a reminder of her Spanish mother and her childhood in South America Marlene speaks German, not with a foreign accent but in a special way. Spanish is really her 'first' language, and she speaks German with Spanish speed. As German words don't lend themselves to this staccato method every now and then she pauses for a moment to get them in order, recapitulates the last words, and on it goes. German in the Spanish fashion.

After her father's death the clan moved to Ibiza and made it their base, to visit or leave as they like. From there Marlene's Chilean brother Tilly (24) makes a journey every few months in his 1951 BMW, often to his sister at Salzburg. Niki likes his brother-in-law and has made a big studio at the top of the house with plenty of light and a view : Tilly paints. At the moment he specializes in forests, first out of his own imagination, then he flew to Malaysia 'to examine nature' and found it was just as he thought 'Whatever you invent – flowers, leaves, trees – it all exists in the jungle.' He says he would be a successful painter and his pictures would fetch a good price, but he is slow and production is therefore limited.

When Lauda first met Marlene and her family his favourite way of describing them was : 'They are all so relaxed.' Relaxed, relaxed, a fascinating idea to the rather tense Niki, who had lived for seven years with a very disciplined young lady. Sometimes the chance observer of Marlene's *relaxed* behaviour has a slight suspicion that it is a little act, put on to make Niki laugh, and break through the strain which he often shows.

One thing is certain : Niki is not *easy*, but he would like to be easy, and he likes people who are easy or pretend to be. That is why people with built-in importance, or racing drivers who want to talk racing, are unsuitable as friends for Lauda. What he needs are types who are not too intellectual, or else contact with them is a strain, and costs 'substance'.

By 'types' Niki means people who are in some way interesting and who don't lose their identity vis à vis the star, or treat him in a special way because he's the famous racing driver. That alone would be too simple; it goes further. The 'type' mustn't knuckle under to him, but he must naturally know how to behave with him, in an unobtrusive way. For example 'Bertl', a jolly KTM employee and friend of the millionaire Walter Wolf. Bertl has no special function for Lauda, which is an enormous advantage, because he doesn't have to be a bore with wanting this or that. And then : 'Bertl is a personality, and if I swear at him, he doesn't say I'm sorry Herr Lauda but just swears at me. Bertl isn't the only one, specially among pilots I know lots of people who treat me just like anyone else. That's why I like going to the pilots' place in Salzburg airport.'

Bertl Wimmer, without any special function, went round almost the whole Grand Prix circus this year, sometimes as a Wolf satellite and sometimes as a Lauda man. Lauda seemed to want very much to have Bertl nearby, and took a lot of trouble (meeting, transport, hotel bookings). A man from his troupe who lost his passport in New York would normally get a growl of 'Should have looked out' from Lauda, but for Bertl he busied himself personally with the problem.

Three or four of these men, all perfectly 'natural' down-to-earth and entertaining, are Lauda's best friends; despite Niki's dislike of the word 'friend'. Sometimes he says he's got no friends, he asks for a definition of the word friend. 'What is a friend ?' and says in a perplexed way 'Call all my acquaintances friends if you like'. Behind that there is obviously the mistrust and the anxiety of a man who doesn't want to be exploited. For example, he had an acquaintance who for years could call himself Lauda's 'friend'. But Lauda had less and less time for him and was really angry when the man said : 'Why did you give an interview saying you had no friends? I am after all your friend !' Because of this sort of thing Lauda sweeps the word under the carpet. Bertl, Schurl, Helmut, he likes them, he's pleased to see them, and that's enough.

Money, decorations and rank are not very interesting to Lauda. His indifference to celebrities who are presented to him on a golden platter is real, without pretence or coquetry. It sometimes interests him to meet a famous person to see what impression he makes, but that is enough, the case is disposed of, the man doesn't interest him further. Lauda has got nothing against Prince Rainier and Princess Grace of Monaco, but as a privileged person he feels no special desire to get to know them. If his driving would benefit even in the smallest degree because he refused to dine with the Prince, Lauda would stay in his hotel room, as in 1977, when he felt during training rather below par and wanted to build himself up. And for building him up Willy Dungl is better than the Prince, and therefore there's no question about Lauda's choice. When he was asked if he wasn't disappointed to have missed an evening with Rainier, he said : 'I have no idea what the Prince is like. His social life doesn't interest me. Perhaps I shall discover one day that he is a kind and sympathetic character, and then it would be fine to get to know him better. But meanwhile I should spend my time more sensibly if I went to the canteen and had a beer with Maurer Schurl.'

Lauda likes Walter Wolf, the multi-millionaire, but says : 'Not because of his money, and not even because of his success as a self-made man.' He has never admired people for being rich, and this goes for his own family too. With Wolf it is once again the 'type' he likes. 'People think he's an arrogant fool, but he's got a good heart and I like the way he looks at motor racing. He can't even pronounce Cosworth, he says Cosmot, and when he means Brabham he says Braaa-ham. He has got an unusual way with problems and I like seeing what he does. When I know he's doing something silly I tell him my opinion. Perhaps he'll pay attention, perhaps he won't.'

Although he values professional know-how in people he works with, he dislikes motor racing gossip. Other drivers don't interest him in the least, with the exception of James Hunt, but then he is a 'type'. For a time he thought he liked Jody Scheckter, but that soon ended. Lauda is an introvert, and that is part of the reason for his minimal contact with other racing drivers – the younger Formula I drivers he hasn't even *met*, for example his successor at Ferrari's, the Canadian Gilles Villeneuve : 'I can't say anything about him, I don't know him.' Asked about racing driver cliques, or even friendships (such as Jackie Stewart – Jochen Rindt – Piers Courage) he says : 'In those days racing drivers had an easier life. There were fewer races, much less testing, one simply had more time. If I have five minutes to myself I would rather see my wife than any racing driver. Those drivers who all lived near each other in Switzerland, each on a different hill, sat in the sun and looked at the Geneva lake, Rindt was bored, Stewart was bored, Courage was bored too, so they all sat there together. But now unfortunately there's no time to be bored.'

That there are many things one could say about that, changes nothing. Each person lives in his own way, and Niki loves his snail-shell house very much. A certain reserve, in some ways isolation, is in his nature, and he's not concerned to change this. He won't even change when he's an ex-World Champion, and less famous. Marlene says Niki will open up if he's taken in the right way, but he : 'Opening up is difficult for me, sometimes even with my own wife.'

Interest in the houses of racing drivers dates from the book on Stirling Moss,* in which Ken Purdy describes Moss's house so enthusiastically that I asked Moss for an interview, just in order to see inside this remarkable house. Moss took great trouble and used sophisticated methods so that he could live in the very middle of London and yet live quietly. His house is near enough to the Hilton to be able to use its television aerial, and yet it has the luxury of a little garden. Even fifteen years ago there was a video camera at the entrance, which turns on when the bell rings and throws a picture of the visitor on every television screen in the five storey house. This was the first of an orgy of electronic gadgets which Moss enjoys showing.

Lauda's house is not so unusual. There are no gadgets or gags – except that fireproof under-pants spin around in the washing-machine, but in this case that's normal. The huge house, ten kilometres east of Salzburg, looks almost like an hotel from the road, so plain and severe, but it improves as you get near. The site is unbeatable; at the back a hill, a view in every direction, eastward to the Fuschl lake. Fields all round, and on one side the forest comes up to the kitchen window. The only neighbour, a hundred metres away and lying lower down, is a farm which belongs to Enzinger-Wastl, who likes going to his neighbour's races, where of course he sits in the Lauda pits. When Niki became World Champion Wastl came down handsomely and marched in with a live sow for a present.

Despite the proximity of the high road and a motor road (though divided by a valley) getting to the house is not too easy. The last hundred metres are a private road with three notices forbidding entry – there is no fence or railings. That would spoil the view, Niki thinks, and protection from sight-seers will soon not be necessary any more – 'when I stop racing nobody will bother about me.'

That originally there was an idea of making a proper entrance is shown by the existence of a door in the right place,

* *All but my Life,* by Stirling Moss and Ken Purdy, William Kimber 1963.

with a footpath leading to it. In practice everyone goes through the garage. The garage was to have its own car washing apparatus, (Niki is disgusted by dirty cars) but in fact Gustl, of whom more later, washes the cars. The idea that a garage for four cars would suffice the Lauda family soon became a ridiculous absurdity. The list at the end of October 1977 : one 1961 Bentley (Niki : 'I only have it because I like old well-kept cars. I hardly ever drive it, because otherwise people think I'm Udo Jürgens') one Jaguar XJ 12 5.3 with telephone, one Alfetta GT with telephone, one Fiat 132 2-litre, one Alfasud Kombi, one Volkswagen beetle cabrio (Marlene's car). Then there's a Honda 550 and a KTM. Add the housekeeper's Vauxhall and the Scirocco belonging to Luigi, with one or two visitors's cars, and the place looks like a car park. The 'second car' is more like a 'seventh car', and that would be the Ferrari 308 GTB which he had the use of until the end of his contract, but which Lauda scarcely ever used, (a beautiful car, but too much of a strain. Formula I World Champions prefer to drive in silent automatic limousines.)

Lauda's cars must always be clean and perfect in every detail. When it comes to cars Lauda is very fussy; a broken radio in one of the six puts him in a bad mood; the thought that for today he can choose one of the other five is no help. As in winter the conditions on the roads sometimes make the use of any of the cars impossible a Range Rover became a necessity, which meant parting with the beloved Jaguar (he would never spend *money* on a car, except for the Bentley which is more of a toy than anything else). For the ordinary driver it may be interesting to know by what criteria the most competent driver in the world judges his cars. 1. The functioning of the motor-telephone. 2. The quality of the stereo installation. 3. Quiet running. 4. Seat comfort. 5. Design of the body. That details like engine performance, road-holding and brakes come up to standard are taken as a matter of course. These priorities show

how Lauda's driving habits have changed. (a) He flies in his private Jet if at all possible, (b) he drives much more sensibly than two or three years ago (in those days he looked upon driving as part of his training, especially in Italy where he called the oncoming traffic 'the third Monza chicane'). Today he uses driving time to telephone (he can get through to anywhere in the world by pressing a few buttons) or listening to music.

You get into the house through the garage, which takes up the whole of one side, then by the boiler room and a sort of workshop to a little hall. Straight on are the guest rooms, the dog's room, Marlene's darkroom, a Sauna and finally out to the swimming pool. However the usual thing is to go from the hall upstairs to the first floor, the main floor. When about six steps from the top the biggest dog in Austria appears on the landing and gets ready to give the visitor's face a good licking. It is useless to try and fend off the friendliness of the Great Dane with your hands. As soon as the dog allows you to get by you are in the ante-room. In the direction of the swimming pool are the bedrooms, on the other side the drawing room. There are passages to the study and the kitchen. The stairs lead up to another floor, but over the drawing room there is only a balcony, because it goes right up to the roof. The rest of the top floor has got more visitors' rooms and bathroom, and a big room which Tilly uses as a studio when he is there.

The centre of the house is the large drawing room, which is divided into veranda, a place round the fire, and a dining room. It gets its effect from its height and the huge picture window with a view over fields and forests and the lake. In describing this living-room you are struck by the mixture of styles which in the ordinary way would not go together, but here they give an impression of generosity and comfort and good living. The system behind it all must have been lovingly thought out – certainly not by Niki, who enjoys the result but had no hand in the decoration. The boldest thing is the gold-coloured dining room furniture. The spick and span brass might seem too cold-looking, but together with all the rest it goes well.

Where the walls are not glass they are covered with pictures, small pictures, about fifty of them, water colours, drawings, a few reproductions of famous works, otherwise originals by the Knaus family, either Marlene's father or her brother Tilly. Subjects and technique are distinguishable, but the arrangement is not planned, it is the whole impression which counts. Pretty, interesting, bold, superior – as you like it.

From the dining-room a door leads to the kitchen, which has got all the automatic gadgets, naturally, but above all a huge window, with pine trees right up to it. An ideal place in which to fry a schnitzel.

The size of the dining-room table (six places) shows the limit of Lauda's dinner parties. Although there is room for ten people to stay in the house, Lauda says: 'That's only for extreme emergencies.'

When the Laudas are in their living room there's always gramophone music. As the loudspeakers are at the level of the top storey the whole room is filled with sound, mostly background music. Soft Pop of the top class, almost Jazz, carefully chosen. Lauda's number one is Randy Newman, then Bill Withers, Rod Stewart and Stevie Wonder. If classical music is played in Lauda's house, that is exclusively for Marlene.

A television (with Video apparatus) stands there but is not often turned on. The shelf near it is full of video tapes, the transmissions of all the races carefully labelled. The titles of the cassettes are among the few things in the room which betray the profession of its owner. There are also motor sport books on the shelves, and two photographs of Niki in overalls (not in winning pose, just grinning in a friendly way) but no trophy of any description disturbs the idyll of the well-off ordinary citizen.

Niki's study points to his profession and his hobby, particularly the new hobby, photographs of airplanes take up more space than those of cars; the place of honour is for Marlene. The writing table – made of massive glass supported by metal legs – is usually covered with a few papers, as though there were some matters to be cleared up, but not too much. Near the writing-table stands the only cup in the entire house – it is from the race at Jarama in 1974, Lauda's first Grand Prix win. Niki won't allow that it is there for sentimental reasons connected with his first win, he says it's so practical for hanging things like elastic bands and scissors on its elaborate surface. And all sorts of things dangle from this sumptuous goblet.

All the rest of the cups and goblets, bowls, pots, statues, smoking appliances, dinner services, pictures, glass, reproductions and sculptures his successes in ten years of motor racing have brought him have disappeared. Sometimes Lauda has simply left them behind, or given them away on the spot, sometimes they have gone to acquaintances – or to Gustl.

Gustl is the leaseholder of the Shell petrol station at the east end of the little town of Hof, hardly two kilometres away from Lauda's house. Where other filling stations put accessories on show, Gustl has got original trophies won by the World Champion, and on the day after Lauda's win at Hockenheim his clients came with the usual request : 'Show us the new cup !' Since Gustl has got so many goblets he leaves his two Alsatians in the filling station at night, which Lauda says is taking too much trouble : 'They're not all that important.' In return for the trophies Lauda's cars all get washed at Gustl's filling station, and very carefully polished because the Champ is so particular about it. Fair exchange : both sides profit from the prizes of motor racing.

Lauda tried once or twice to use his cups, for instance as a bowl for the dog's dinner. But most of the trophies are so covered in decorations that the dog has great difficulty getting the last scraps of meat.

LAUDA : 'The things are useless because one gets nothing but muck. Two or three of them appeal to me, and I've asked Ghedini to keep them for me, I'll fetch them some time. For example in America I was given a huge silver bowl, quite plain, you could put something in it, flowers perhaps. But ninety per cent of all the prizes are useless and therefore worthless. You might just as well give a rotten potato as you shake hands and say hearty congratulations on your victory. At every race it's different, but sometimes you stand there with your arms full of goblets and then an old man pushes through from the back and puts one more bowl on you. You are simply bombarded with trash, there's no sense or feeling of honour about it, and that's why I think nothing of cups and only keep them when they mean something : either because they are beautiful or else because they're useful – but that's very very seldom.'

He was completely puzzled by a gift he got as winner of the Grand Prix in Holland in 1977, a small square stone with beads stuck on it in the shape of a car, and some signatures. It was utter trash and Lauda was just going to throw it away when someone said there might be some real diamonds among the beads, which would be worth a few hundred thousand schillings. So Lauda put the object on a shelf, to remind himself of it. It is still there today, and Niki says to Marlene about once a week : 'We must get a jeweller to look at it.' And Marlene agrees.

If his attitude to prizes – and every sort of honour and cere-monial – shows that Lauda is a *practical* man, it is quite true, he is. The masseur Willy Dungl was struck by something typical at one of the races. Lauda had won the Dutch Grand Prix 1977, and let all the usual honours flow over him, without much pleasure, and showed only for one single detail spontaneous joy. It was when the police who were escorting his car to the air-port in Amsterdam took him along a one-way street in the wrong direction, in order to avoid a traffic jam. Then he was really enthusiastic, it was *worth* something. There was some point in winning the Grand Prix if you could go the wrong way along a one-way street, that is so to speak not just an empty ceremony but an honour of practical value.

A central, almost a dominant role in the Lauda household is played by the dog. Lauda originally wanted a Boxer, but he was pleased when Marlene came home in the spring of 1976 with a Great Dane puppy. It was given the name Baghira because of the resemblance to a panther, black with white flecks on paws, front and tail. Baghira grew according to plan into a giant dog, which Niki finds okay. A big place, a big house and a big dog. Lauda loves the animal, spends a lot of time with him and gets into a panic when Baghira runs away – especially since one of the keepers said 'next time' he would shoot the dog. Lauda rushes out and drives to the spot where he is most afraid of the keeper. The thought that the dog might meet with an accident comes to him sometimes for no particular reason. Once he was describing the psychological stress within the Ferrari team, the war of nerves, and when he wanted to give a really telling example he said, 'It is almost as if someone whispered in my ear just before the start of a race : Your dog is dead.'

The playfulness and the high spirits of this young animal bring life into the house, the dog is all over the place. Niki declares that Baghira is fairly well-trained (except for licking the guests, which he can't be stopped from doing). Marlene's Volkswagen Cabrio has over the months had all its inside pulled out, Baghira eats everything from the upholstery to the dashboard, though he wouldn't behave like this in the Jaguar, and he very seldom bites the Fiat.

The house is looked after by Marlene and a housekeeper, and often Niki's childhood friend Luigi is there too, as a 'working guest' in the role of honorary caretaker. The land belonging to the house is only partly kept up, a few flower beds near the garage and round the swimming pool, Marlene's little kitchen garden – the rest is left to nature, except that Wastl sometimes mows the meadows.

The peace of country life is only disturbed by the telephone. Guests are rare, because Lauda greatly values the house for its quiet and snail-shell quality. Therefore he much prefers seeing people in Salzburg, and meeting in neutral surroundings to talk business rather than having them at home. He is particularly averse to being photographed at home – the two or three pictures were only taken for his book, or in return for huge sums of 'pain money', and even that, he says, wouldn't make him pose at home in future. His public life stops at the frontier of his property.

Invitations to the 'inner circle' to stay the night, for example to the Montezemolo clan, Ghedini and Helmut Marko, depend on Niki's mood. Basically he is hospitable, but then he gets in a panic 'when it's like an hotel' and he throws everyone out, even Luigi.

He has been named an 'honoured citizen' of the parish of Hof (even though he spends so much of the year travelling) and Lauda is a great attraction there, but everyone knows it irritates him not to be treated in a 'normal' way. He takes part in parish life, sometimes goes to the pub, or to one of the farmers, and also to the forest festival, and he patiently submits once a year to a ceremony in honour of the World Champion, attended by politicians and, for example, to celebrate a newly-opened *Raiffeisenkasse*.

So we have a very everyday picture of a perfect idyll in the unbeatable surroundings of one of the loveliest places in Europe, ten minutes by motor-road from Salzburg and from the airport. The reward for his hard work is very evident. What value does he put upon money and possessions?

LAUDA : 'Naturally it is lovely to live in nice surroundings.

But I don't depend on material things. If tomorrow I could never drive again and was out of the business, and if at the same time the house burnt down, I should live in a little flat just as I did for many years. It wouldn't wreck my life if I had to give up my possessions. It is in my nature to work hard and to do my utmost. If I were a shoemaker I should try to be a damned good shoemaker, and I should be satisfied with that, I shouldn't dream of Onassis's yacht. Earning a lot of money is automatically bound up with success in motor racing. That is pleasant, but it's not what counts.'

Niki, tell how you picture to yourself a perfect day in your private life, a day without any work.

'Days with no work, I mean without any work whatsoever, are terribly rare. How such a day goes would depend principally on whether I was plus or minus. If I were minus, and hadn't recovered from the exertions of the last days, it couldn't be a perfect day. I should wander around, and only want to rest or sleep as much as possible. When I am rested I get up about nine, look at the papers, have a leisurely breakfast, telephone someone like Bertl or Helmut and ask whether they'd like to come motor bicycling with me. On the Honda I relax. If I know we are going to drive around further I get myself up in leather jacket and helmet and all the rest, and so I am incognito, even if a few people think they recognize the helmet. On those days we drive all round the Salzkammergut, even as far as Linz. We drive pretty fast.

'Or else I see only Marlene, and do everything she wants to do, because usually I can do much too little for her. Of course the dog comes into one of those days too, I can walk for hours with him. Sometimes when I want to give him a good run I accompany him on the KTM. Then there are the local farmers, I visit them. Then there's the pilots' canteen at Salzburg airport, where I like to go in the late afternoon for a beer. And then I've got plenty to do. I've been learning about flying for years, it goes on and on, endlessly.'

The longing that famous people have for peace and quiet in life – according to Lauda there are only a few days in the year when he gets them. In the majority are the hectic days, the days when he is *minus* and becomes more *minus* still. The decisive thing here is sleep.

NIKI : 'The days following a race are the most hectic. The night after the race I usually sleep badly, and sometimes I take sleeping pills, but I don't want to depend on them. I ought to take two whole days off to rest, and then on Wednesday I should be fit again, but that never happens. An example : Monday to Vienna for television, Tuesday some test or other for which I have to get the airplane at 6 a.m.; in between, the office, appointments, discussions, interviews and so on and so forth.

Suddenly it's too much for me, and I say *enough, enough, enough* and cancel the next appointments. I know exactly the borderline of getting over-stretched, I know it by the way I sleep. When I only sleep four or five hours a night and that begins to seem the normal amount, it's getting critical. Different people have different needs – as far as I go it is wrong to live in such a way that I only get five hours' sleep, because I need between eight and ten hours. If I wake up too early I have to force myself to rest. Then I lie down in the afternoon and sleep three hours like a king. After that of course I am fit, and run round with the dog or go into the Sauna, and that makes me tired and I have another good sleep. That is how I get back to "normal". In the last year it's become ever harder to get enough time to recover strength.'

What the business man or the over-strained person can learn from Lauda is to draw the limits, to know how far body and nerves can be stretched, and the consequences of the counter-measures. This man, sometimes called a computer, studies his own physique as carefully as possible. He knows that his much-prized intellect becomes worthless the moment the primitive bodily functions cease to work. The clear analysis of the body-and-mind situation at any given time is at least one component of the often repeated opinion, that Lauda thinks more than do other Grand Prix drivers.

The man behind the unbelievably successful treatment after Lauda's injuries in the two accidents (the tractor, and the Nürburgring) is the Viennese masseur Willy Dungl, aged forty. His diagnosis : 'Lauda is not the type of top athlete, he has the muscles of the average man. The reason that he can nevertheless achieve extraordinary results is his self-discipline, and his readiness to undertake endurance training. Four weeks after the Nürburgring accident he was still very weak when we took the first soundings. Already after five days' training he was improving, and when a week later he was examined by the medical commission in Milan he did the so-called stair test and held out longer than the voice of the announcer one-two-three. Of course we had perfect circumstances for building him up in the sea air on Ibiza, and therefore the doctors' commission did not worry him.

'Lauda always has to know *why*,' says Dungl. 'When he understands the reason for something he can accomplish the impossible. If you can't explain what this or that exercise is going to do towards the target, he doesn't help. For example he doesn't much like exercises, he is not the type for them. But after the time in Spain in 1977 when he was unable to start the race it was obvious to me that we should have to strengthen the muscles between the ribs. When I had explained this he accepted to do strengthening exercises and did them almost to the point of self-destruction. He is a marvellous patient for a masseur, because he has the gift of completely relaxing in a short space of time. He can relax so much between two periods of training that you can massage every single muscle.'

Lauda does not want to depend on anyone, whether it be the fitness-guru Günther Traub or the masseur. Apart from one great building-up programme each year and a few routine checks he only gets hold of Dungl when the situation is critical. But the Brazilian doctor Grajales is a fixture at all the Grand Prix races. Grajales, who originally worked for Fittipaldi, is now always available for Lauda. His job is to know exactly all about the hospitals in the district, the diverse possibilities at the clinics, the availability of any specialists who may be needed, and to be ready for any emergency.

It is remarkable the way Lauda sets his face against Parkinson's Law : 'Get a writing table and work will follow.' Lauda turns this round : 'Every secretary you don't employ saves you time.'

Lauda Incorporated is organized as follows : Niki has a cousin, Jenzy, who has an office in Salzburg. There's a girl in the office who knows Lauda's business extremely well and where everything is. Messages can be left there, and requests. They are dealt with from time to time. Lauda hasn't even got proper writing paper, just a blank sheet with his name typed at the top, and his signature at the bottom – isn't that enough? In this way only important things are dealt with. The unimportant just bounce off this system, or lack of system.

It is amusing to compare Lauda with Jochen Rindt in this regard. Jochen was also an informal type, and he had lived a long time on the Geneva lake before he was really on top, yet his correspondence was always dealt with by a solicitor in Vienna.

Niki's system of dealing with everyday matters in the simplest, most informal and painless fashion has got one small gap. He is naturally a credit-card man and tries on journeys to pay everything by credit card. He only has the Diners Club card and manages well with it all over the world, and yet not a hundred per cent. In some cases he needs American Express. In 1970 or 1971 Lauda tried to join American Express and also Diners Club. Diners accepted, Amexco did not – the reason being the bad bank report, because at that time Lauda was heavily over-drawn.

Since then the minus is a thing of the past and Amexco would certainly accept him, but he cannot bring himself to ask. 'Now', he argues, 'I should be doing them a favour in using their card, because it's good for Amexco if Lauda pays with Amexco.'

So he remains firm and punishes Amexco for their lack of trust; ('Certainly my bank account was in a bad way, but if they had been any good they would have been more flexible. A certain risk is inevitable in this business.') So he punishes himself : 'I always get angry when someone says no, sorry, we don't take Diners Club, but of course you've got an American Express card? Then I have to change money or write a cheque, both a waste of time.'

About time : in private and in public Lauda is punctual. He doesn't forgive unpunctuality in others. Sometimes this leads to a heightening of the usual hectic tension, because he makes appointments one after another to get them over as quickly as possible. At the worst you can reckon with a telephone call : 'Sorry, I shall be ten minutes late.' The good manners of this example cannot be denied. Marlene : 'He has made me punctual.'

The unavoidable question : What hobbies has a World Champion got? Flying, he says, is his only hobby. Otherwise he finds motor bicycling relaxing, and he would like to go ski-ing except that the value of his bones is so prohibitively high. Music, he says, but only by the way. Otherwise everything fits in with the idea of the 'new man', the 'computer generation'. The one-sidedness, the lack of interest in almost everything non-technical. And the question already posed by Helmut Zwickl, when he asked the Clark-Gurney-Surtees generation : 'Are there still green trees for you, and sunsets; do you feel that music is beautiful and a book interesting and instructive?' Niki would probably answer : 'Sunsets are okay as long as they don't dazzle too much, I can feel music is beautiful, for the interesting book I've no time.'

Racing motor sport and all that goes with it simply leaves him no time for anything else, unless it be flying. Niki was never many-sided, even before flying ate up his spare time. He considers it's a fact that there's no time left over from sport and flying for anything else. He doesn't have the feeling that he is missing things, he regrets nothing; but he does say that it's possible, after he has retired, that he might get interested in theatres and concerts, that he might read books, but none of this worries him in the least.

When in November 1977 we wrote the last lines of this book, Niki was just about to take his exam for a professional pilot's instrument flying certificate; in barely four years he has concentrated on his hobby in such a way it has become serious, and flying will be his life work when he leaves motor racing. This is what the journalist Helmut Zwickl, himself a pilot, has to say about Lauda's flying ability :

> You can see in the way he flies that he is in the world champion class, because he so quickly understands the most complicated instruments, and his gift of quick comprehension and his ability to concentrate are quite out of the ordinary. That is to say, even as a simple private plane pilot he has reached the niveau (though not the experience) of an air-line pilot. His reflexes are so rapid that even in the most unexpected simulated emergency he always intuitively does the right thing.

He mastered the small jet aircraft in the same almost violent way as he forced himself to the top in Formula I – except that this time he had his own money and the fame of his name to help him, under the supervision of top pilots from the Cessna 150 to the Citation, to dash forward to the second stage when he hadn't yet got the first stage behind him. The technique of his whole life has been to choose a suit that is too big for him and then grow into it all the quicker.

Though in other ways he rations and sells his time by the minute, when it comes to flying Lauda measures his time quite differently. A Polsterer man rings to ask whether he would like to go to Morocco as second pilot in a charter flight. In five seconds Lauda ticks off the appointments he would have to cancel, and then accepts–incomprehensible to anyone not bitten by the flying bug. He is attracted to flying the whole time, even if it's only to gossip in an airport canteen. And however restless he sometimes is on the ground, in the air the restlessness disappears at once, and his spirits rise a couple of octaves. He cannot explain his love of flying very well, at any rate not to those for whom the airplane is only the means to an end. (Lauda will drop everything just to fly round Salzburg airport.) 'The more difficult it becomes technically the more attracted I am by flying. The more instruments an airplane has, the more I feel I must get to understand them. It's a question of completely mastering the medium, nothing more.'

Walter Wolf and his helicopter sometimes worry him. 'I'll go for a whole afternoon's autographing to St Koloman (Wolf's home town) if you will give me two hours helicopter lessons.' He says, 'I go mad when I can't master the thing. I get into situations where I have to say 'take it over, otherwise we shall crash' – and that infuriates me. It's not that I can't fly the thing. I can take off, and land.' And he explains with his hands and his feet, vivaciously like a little Formula Ford driver describing how for the first time he managed to pass another driver.'

Flying for flying's sake; he can do it wherever he has to go, which is a good side-effect of his work. Geography is just as abstract in flying as it is in motor racing where you drive for hours getting nowhere. Here a flying-lane, there a chicane, there are special terms for both, but basically they might be anywhere, it makes no difference. The same applies to the country where the races take place; *where* a Grand Prix is run means nothing; the environment, the city, the country are abstract and interchangeable. Only the climate changes : March at Kyalami, January in Buenos Aires, you are reminded every moment that you are in a hot climate. Lauda likes good hotels (Kyalami) and notices dreary ones (Mosport, Canada) he likes Zeltweg best (shortest distance) and Tokyo least (for that he has to take an airliner with all the annoyance of waiting, booking places, being in a crowd, customs and restricted space.) Otherwise the wide world is all the same to him; he avoids Niagara Falls even if he is going within three kilometres of it, and he refuses to go up the highest tower in the world in Toronto. 'Why should I go up the highest tower in the world and then just think about the race, what's the point?'

Automobile World Champion Andreas Nikolaus Lauda, symbol of the technical age. He likes movement, he likes flying, he doesn't like journeys.

It is unusual for Lauda to relax completely, but it happens sometimes. Then he drinks wine and whisky and smokes dreadful cigarillos non-stop, they look like burnt grass stalks and taste sweet. At such times he is ready for anything. The computer rejects its programme. Such occasions never happen when he's on the job, after a Grand Prix for example, and there's never a special reason for them. Lauda doesn't say, 'Today we'll celebrate my World Champion title.' The atmosphere on Ibiza makes him high-spirited, and Marlene is enthusiastic about the way her Niki relaxes there; sometimes he dances all night.

MARLENE : 'He is a good dancer, with a charm of his own in

his movements. Sometimes, like a boy, he is embarrassed when people stare. I love his way of dancing.'

Not only for Marlene but also for friends and acquaintances who see him often the Nürburgring accident is over and done with. If you are often with Lauda you just don't notice the burns on his face, you get so used to the parchment-like skin on part of it. Only the remarks of outsiders are a reminder that Lauda's face is 'different'. In this way it is easy to imagine that the results of the accident don't matter to him in the slightest; he is quite used to his new face, and he notices that as the months go by the new skin gets more and more like the unburnt skin. He plans no more cosmetic operations, doesn't worry over his burnt ear, which in any case is hidden in his long hair, as is the skin of his head which in the beginning was so badly burnt.

What results of the accident remain?

Niki himself has already answered in this book; he says he is tougher, more mature, more deliberate.

And Marlene, does she see a difference? 'Yes, his body is sturdier, Niki is more strongly built than formerly. Even his character is stronger, more mature. He doesn't shut himself up as much as he used to, he is easier with people, he is generally in a better mood than before. Whatever changes the accident made, they are all for the better.'

So 1st August 1976 is totally disposed of.

Lauda has not thought about his retirement, at least not about the timing of it. He lets things go along, and works at his 'second leg', flying, with all its professional possibilities, as entrepreneur, promoter or pilot. From the style of his behaviour hitherto one must expect a surprise when he retires.

NIKI : 'I can easily imagine that at some time I might make a sudden decision, overnight, zack zack.'

When Jackie Stewart retired there was a gala dinner in

London with four hundred guests and Princess Anne and a crowd of famous people. How does Niki picture his farewell party? 'The same sort of thing, only with four instead of four hundred. And instead of the Princess I shall probably invite Bertl or Schurl, because I like them. But I don't really know yet.'

PART THREE

The Early Years

Is there something to be learnt from this account of a career, is there a spark of how-I-became-a-millionaire wisdom in it? In a certain sense there is, but the receipt is not one you can follow; it only works in this country, at this moment in time, with this particular man, with his toughness, his thoroughness.

The word that witnesses of his career use most often about Lauda is 'unobtrusive'. This is probably because the almost violent compulsion which took him on from one stage to the next was hidden within an outwardly calm young man. He reminds one of a gambler who is forever on the verge of losing all, and then doubles his stake at the last moment. And he uses the money he hopes to win in the next round for this doubled stake.

The background of his parents' house: Lauda undoubtedly got manners and style from it. It can never be certain whether the name Lauda, which belongs to one of Austria's leading families, was not perhaps decisive three or four times, in helping his early backers to make up their minds. And then an ordinary village boy would never have had the imagination to get into debt and plan on a world scale, as he did from the very beginning. This is all hypothesis and Niki adds: 'I might have taken a year longer if I'd been an ordinary village boy, if I'd had the determination – but then perhaps I shouldn't have had the determination.' In any case, where the ordinary beginner thinks in thousands, for Niki it was tens of thousands, and they didn't belong to him. Thinking in such generous terms can be explained rather by his background than by an inclination for confidence tricks, or lack of seriousness.

The fact that Niki's family had no understanding or sympathy for his racing career and gave him very little cash, does not alter the advantage his family name was to him at the outset, particularly in Vienna with its complex cliques of the rich and powerful.

If you press Niki to describe his childhood, he first remembers a scene which he already put in his first book.*

> Even when it wasn't all that cold I had to wear a scarf and coat and put on a Styrian hat. My brother was always identically dressed, we looked two complete nitwits. I can see it all so vividly still : there I am eleven or twelve years old and paying frequent visits to the dentist who's straightening my teeth out. I'm standing with my mother on the corner by the Forum cinema waiting for the tram. I just keep looking at this manhole cover – each time a car goes over it it wobbles, click-clack. And if I visualise now how must I have looked standing there in my coat and scarf and hat on that corner – I must have looked a real *Seicherl,* a softy.

What else can you remember?

'Clop clop clop, a horse coming out of its loose box. I learnt to ride, as was usual in our sort of family. Every time I went to the riding-school the smell disgusted me. And when the horse was brought out and I heard the clop clip I felt ill. I peed in my pants and rushed upstairs to the lavatory.'

* Niki Lauda, The Art and Science of Grand Prix Driving (Osceola, Wis.: Motorbooks International, 1977).

He must then have been about ten; he overcame his dislike later on and learnt to ride perfectly, as a Lauda should. He tried it again when he grew up, it went quite well, but not so well as to make him do it often.

For the nineteen-year-old, getting into motor sport meant opposition from his family and difficulties over money, not to mention school: he was due to matriculate at high school. However he apeared on the scene in the spring of 1968 with a well-prepared Mini Cooper S, for which he owed 40,000 schillings. This debt was to be paid out of his prize money, so one may say Lauda believed in Lauda. The Mini was designed for mountain races, and at that time in Austria mountain races were a suitable discipline as preparation for bigger things.

Lambert Hofer, five years older than Lauda and like him from the Vienna *jeunesse dorée,* saw him close up during his first season.

'You couldn't take him seriously when he said he'd bought the Mini Cooper. He had no spare parts, no mechanic, no trailer, not even a shed. The Mini was kept in the Potzleinsdorf garage where it looked terribly out of place. Niki had plenty of time, he had done his exams more or less and hung about my garage a lot, where two mechanics were working on my car. He was a perfectly ordinary fan, he read all the motor sport papers, loved talking about it and was obsessed by races like all of us. For his first mountain race his uncle lent him an eight cylinder BMW to tow the Mini. I went home after the training and heard then that he was second in his class (up to 1300 cm 3).

'What struck me was that Niki came back and said he would probably have won if he had fully used the whole available rev band. The former owner of the Mini Cooper had advised him not to go above 8000 revolutions, which he had done instead of the usual 9000. That amazed me, to think this crazy young man was so disciplined that he could take the advice he'd been given. I can't imagine any other beginner in his position being so careful of his car.

'The typical Lauda of those days was unobtrusive. What distinguished him from most of his motor racing contemporaries were his good manners, which he got from his home. Most of the other boys from rich families – Quester and many others – were quite a bit older, and a stage or two ahead of him. In his age group he was the only 'rich boy' but he mixed well with all the others, who were naturally louder and rougher than he was.'

In the next three mountain races Lauda just managed to win in his class. He was fast but not sensational, only a tenth of a second faster than the other Austrians with similar cars. In the middle of the season Lauda exchanged the not yet paid-for Mini Cooper S with an even less paid-for Porsche 911. As security for it a glance at his parents' villa sufficed.

LAMBERT HOFER: 'It was typical of those days that the car of the moment was always his own possession, and even this "possession" was loaded with debt. One single accident and that would have been the end. None of these boys could get anyone to insure them. But there was never the slightest doubt among the people who believed in him that Lauda would pay his debts sometime. With the Porsche 911 the situation was critical. Niki from the very beginning was a perfectionist and wanted only the best. So he got Gerhard Mitter to tune the 911, and ordered optimal treatment.

'It sometimes happened that he couldn't fetch the car because he hadn't enough money for the bill. Then he had to think of some other way of borrowing and got deeper into debt. We used to do long distance races together. He was a good partner, reliable and clever. The risk was just the same for me, everything I possessed was in the car, and if he or I had piled it up that would have been the end. For a race at Nürburgring we trained a whole week. One drove and the other sat by him and then we changed round after a few laps, but usually in between the passenger was sick.'

The 911 brought in enough so that Lauda could drive in 1969 for Kurt Bergmann's Formula V Team ('Karimann'). At the beginning of the season Lauda had his first accident, at the airport race at Aspern bei Wien. Lauda's recollection : 'I was crazy, and so set on driving, too much so, and I didn't think, I just wanted to pass where it wasn't possible, like Andretti, and I turned a somersault.'

Whether this first accident made him feel frightened, he cannot remember. He only knows he wanted to go right on driving, to correct his mistake.

Austria's latest Formula I driver Helmut Marko remembers the time when he first noticed Lauda : 'It was at a very un-important mountain race, we were both in the Kaimann team. He was an unknown lad, but terribly quick in the first train-ing, fastest in fact. When I talked to him it transpired that he had not only been down the mountain before but that he knew every little bump and had noted every bit of uneven surface and so on. In those days he wasn't so close as now and he admitted to me how he got his extra tenth of a second, and I thought then he uses his brain more than the others. He had prepared himself for this little race as though it had been the final of the European mountain championship. So much seriousness was not usual then among young drivers, we were always in such a rush.'

His team manager, Kurt Bergmann, on the twenty-year-old Lauda : 'It certainly wasn't easy for him. Yes, he could drive in Finland but only if he got his own transport for the car. He was the first in Formula V to do the Nürburgring in under 10 minutes, but in the race he got pushed off the track. He was determined to win at Hockenheim, on the last few corners

Breinsberg and he were in the lead in turns three times, until on the last corner Breinsberg cut across his nose and won. "What cheek!" grumbled Breinsberg afterwards, "What the hell did he think he was doing?"

'Lauda knew nothing about the technical side, he had instinct and a very good touch, but he couldn't describe it or build up theories about it. His life was totally given to motor sport. He asked me whether he was a good driver or did I think he would ever be a good racing driver. I had the feeling he might get to the top in Austria, and eventually make a very useful Formula II driver. For anything beyond that there wasn't much sign at the time. For one thing I had a feeling he would never get enough money, finance would be his un-doing, because money was decisive for getting on. He was up to all the tricks and he was unbelievably obstinate with people he hoped to get something from, but all the same I simply didn't see any hope for him to get hold of so much money, as was necessary if you were really going to get on quickly, even in Formula II. He lived very modestly and always wore the same clothes and got himself nothing except what had to do with motor sport, but it wasn't much help.'

About Lauda's style of driving, Bergmann made an interesting observation in those days: 'I saw that every time Lauda got into a higher horse-power class he went better. If modern Formula I cars were only 200 h.p. Lauda wouldn't have been World Champion, but if all Grand Prix cars were 1,000 h.p. he would be even further ahead than he is now. The more it's a question of great power combined with subtle intuition, the further ahead will Lauda be. In this he's the exact opposite of Jochen Rindt, who forced his way through tempestuously.'

1970 was the year when everything in Austrian motor sport revolved round Jochen Rindt, it was the year of his World Champion title and the year of his death. Lauda had brought off another financial coup, he had scratched together sponsors from every possible corner and managed to finance a Porsche 908. Sports car races, he soon found out, were no use on the journey to Formula I, they were a blind alley, with their own laws. The logical way up was: Formula III, Formula II, Formula I. Therefore, Formula III; and Lauda kept up the tremendous pressure to get into the next class, so that he could get into the McNamara Formula III team. It was a year of perfecting himself, and a year of crashes. The first accident happened in the first five minutes of his Formula III career, during the first training at Nogaro in the South of France. He and Pankl were the only Austrians against thirty crazy Frenchmen, so they helped each other during training. Just as Lauda was in the slipstream waiting to cut in and get by the engine of the man in front broke. Lauda with his left front-wheel ran into Pankl's right rear-wheel, catapulted in the air, flew over a marking post, landed on a guard rail, lost all his wheels and skidded for a hundred metres along the rails. 'There was nothing worth mentioning left of the car' remembers Lauda. In the next race – Nürburgring – he simply threw the car away, even now he's not sure why. Then gear box damage in the next, and then Brands Hatch with the typical mistake of a young madcap: he tried to out-brake an opponent, cut the corner, the other knocked his rear wheel, Lauda went off the track, finish.

And then that race early in September at Zolder, which Lauda calls the 'anti-race' of an 'anti-season' and which was a key experience in his career. One day before Jochen Rindt had been killed in an accident at Monza. Lauda describes the Zolder race in his first book :

> That was the maddest thing of all. Third lap : an accident
> – Hannelore Werner – somewhere on the track. We hit the
> brow of the hill in formation at 210 and that's when we find
> the crash-truck barely doing 50. The first three skidded past

it to the right. Hunt made it, so did Birrell. Then another tried to pass on the right, he didn't quite make it and went into a spin. I'm now trying to pass on the left, meantime the other car's spinning to the left, we collide, I turn right round and the next car volleys straight into me. The whole scene takes place slap in the middle of the track, I'm standing there with my car in shreds whe nthe next bunch of cars comes flying over the hill towards us. By now the yellow flag is up and there's all manner of signals, but that mob just kept their foot down. All I could do was sit tight and wonder which side I'd get shot down from first. One flew right over the nose of my car then I jumped out and got the hell out of there.

Lauda analysed the situation and came to the conclusion that he wanted to be a racing driver, with all the consequences, but not a madman in a field of twenty madmen. Formula III was finished as far as he went. A typical Lauda decision followed : he had a rather unsuccessful season, so he doubled his stake; he would get into Formula II.

That was naturally only possible with money, for Lauda had nothing much to boast of – his driving abilty was nothing extraordinary. March needed money – a Formula II season cost about half a million schillings for a man as unknown as Lauda. Niki already played the P.R. game very cleverly, and heaped good references upon the March people. March reckoned to have Lauda as number two behind Peterson, while Niki was running round Austria collecting the money. This time the arrangement didn't work, the needed amount was nowhere near collected.

Nevertheless Lauda signed with March, determined to get the money; what must be, must be. His sponsor Bosch gave one tenth, but the Vienna sport chief at the firm, Count Schönborn, knew the secretary-general of the First Austrian savings-bank, and managed to arrange for Lauda to get credit for a big enough loan. Getting into debt was already part of his life-style, so that was all right.

In this Formula II season with March (1971) Lauda was able for the first time to compare himself with people in the world class. And this meant above all Peterson, because his Swedish colleague in the team was naturally the dominant man in Lauda's world.

Lauda on the Peterson of 1971 : 'He was considered *the* talent, pure and simple. His ability to drive with cars that were handling badly was enormous. He had a quite special gift of driving flat out in all circumstances, but he didn't give himself the trouble of trying to change the circumstances themselves, when they were bad. An example was the Formula II race at Rouen. The March people thought then that our little wing was the right solution, so Ronnie had a small one and I had a bigger one (because only one car had the small wing). In training Ronnie had a better time than I did, mostly because he risked more and drove flat out. In the first round of the race I was surprised to discover that Ronnie couldn't get away from me, without much trouble I kept right up with him (with my bigger wing the car cornered better.)

'Suddenly I got the bold idea, why don't you just overtake the fellow? I waited a while longer, then I passed my number one driver. In the March pits they held out a board for me, saying I should let Peterson by, because then in the second round our star would get the best position. The board would not have been necessary, since Ronnie was so much more experienced and readier to take risks than I was that in any case he would have got me at one of the last corners. All the same they got the impression that I had puposely let Peterson pass me, which gave my image a boost. But the typical part of the situation was that Peterson put up a terrific effort in unfavourable circumstances (the small wing) instead of making the decision to create better circumstances.'

As the year went on Lauda studied Peterson intensively, analysed the reasons for his faster times, reckoned where he could save a tenth of a second, and learnt how to drive flat out, when it was necessary. The season ended with no particular climax, and the money paid to March had gone. But two thirds of the credit remained.

In the autumn Lauda began again to try and get money. It was rather obvious that a medium good Formula II season could not discourage him from once again doubling his stake by getting into Formula I. March offered him a Formula II and Formula I combination for 1972 for a little more than two million schillings. The logical thing for Lauda to do was to raise additional credit. But now the brilliant name of Lauda became for the first time a disadvantage to him. Niki's grandfather went to the president of the bank, who was a friend, and asked him not to give the needful additional credit – 'to bring the boy to his senses'. He succeeded, the savings-bank said no. For Niki that was the final break with his family, but in his career he could not allow any break. In this situation, to remain with only debts and no car would have meant getting a job in order to be able to pay his debts.

The choice of firms was no longer difficult because for the amount of money he needed anything but a bank was out of the question. One of them came across, the *Raiffeisenkasse* gave him a loan of 2.5 million schillings with a life insurance policy as security. Out of that Lauda paid off his debt to the savings-bank; the remainder, a good two million, he took to March. In this way he bought himself a Formula I/Formula II season for the year 1972. Niki Lauda relates :

'March test days at Jarama, a good week before the Spanish Grand Prix. I had two Grand Prix behind me, Argentina and South Africa, an eleventh and a seventh place; I was the little Benjamin of the team, quiet and well-behaved, but a size too small even as Ronnie Peterson's lieutenant. March had brought its new wonder-car, the 721X (with the gears in front of the differential). Ronnie Peterson tested for two whole days, I just had to look on. At the same time Jackie Stewart was testing his Tyrrell. Comparing times, that Peterson was almost as fast as Stewart, the March people became over-confident and euphoric; at last we've got the wonder-car. That Stewart had slid off the road, that during the whole test he'd had problems, was simply swept under the carpet, as well as the possible idea that Jarama might be an unfavourable circuit for the Tyrell.

'The March people only saw that Ronnie was almost as fast as Jackie – and they were overjoyed. In the hotel there was a festive atmosphere; I sat there, I hadn't even been allowed to get into the wonder-car. On the last day I did. They had already told me that there was no defined position for the gear-change, there was a kind of rule of thumb; when there was three fingers' space between the monocoque and the gear lever it was fourth gear, when two fingers it was fifth, there was no spring to stop it moving sideways. I drove away and didn't find the gears and kept changing. After three laps I came in, although I was so terribly anxious to make a good impression and not to make any mistakes. But quite apart from the gears, the car handled frightfully badly, and I couldn't conceive how such muck could possibly race. I drove about fifteen laps and saw no hope, got out and permitted myself to say to Robin Herd : 'I know Ronnie is as fast as Stewart, but if you ask me I just can't get on with the car.' Then spoke March director and designer Robin Herd : 'When you've got as much experience and you can drive as well as Ronnie Peterson, you'll be able to do it too.' He spoke rather slowly and sleepily, I remember every word and it went through and through my brain. I didn't understand myself or the world any more, I had thought I was a good racing driver, but I must have been dreaming.

'For me the car went badly, it jumped about and reacted badly, and Ronnie Peterson said it was a good car, and he drove it as fast as Jackie Stewart. Between these test days and the beginning of practice at Jarama there was a whole week, and I went to Marbella with Mariella for a holiday, to kill time. The entire week what Robin Herd had said went through my head. How could I have got it so wrong? What sort of magician was Ronnie, who could drive so fast with this car, while I couldn't.

'When we came back and both did the official practice in our new cars, it no longer looked quite so marvellous. Peterson only got the ninth best practice time, and I was last, six and a half seconds slower than Jacky Ickx, who was in pole position. For the March people this was no reason to re-think their opinion. They explained Peterson's bad position by trouble with a spin, and my last place needed no explanation, I just couldn't do any better. In the race we both fell out so early that once again no particular reference was drawn about the construction of the 721X.

'The next race was Monaco. That I got position 22 was less painful than Peterson's fifteenth – Peterson, the hero of Monaco, the specialist on this circuit! In the race itself we were eleventh and sixteenth, and Ronnie said for the first time that the car went badly and that it was a catastrophe. Robin Herd was still not convinced, we had to drive the 721X in the next race, the Belgian Grand Prix at Nivelles. But they did put a Hewland gear box in Ronnie's car in place of the usual Alfa, but the fourteenth place in practice was not exactly what was considered suitable for Ronnie Peterson. In these circumstances it wasn't very important that I was once again last, and almost two seconds slower than the next to last. Such superiority in the last places is rare; but no wonder, for I could hardly get round the corners, the thing under-steered so badly. I had often complained to Robin Herd during practice, and once he said : 'I'll do somthing about the under-steering', and had a litre of STP poured into the differential. 'There,' he said, 'now it's all right.' In the race Ronnie and I were so far behind that at last even the most stupid grasped the fact that the March 721X was still-born, a complete dud, a badly constructed car. The type was scrapped.

'I learnt a few lessons from this disaster. The fact that Ronnie Peterson only recognized so late that the car was bad was not a good sign for him. You can't make good such faults by crazy driving, that much was proved. Also my first impression had been right, and from then on I lost all respect for technicians and designers who believe absolutely in their product and want to force everyone else to share their opinion. And then I felt annoyed that I had had self-doubts for a whole week at Marbella, when I was nearly persuaded that I was a not-so-good racing driver. Taking everything together, the 721-X débacle was a toughening experience for me.

'Even the ordinary March, the G model, wasn't up to much that year, not even for Ronnie Peterson. He, the great driving talent of Formula I, was ninth in the world championship; I didn't get a single point.

'I lived on hope for the future. I had good results in Formula II, and with sports cars and touring cars; a lot of people still believed in me, and it looked as if Robin Herd might believe in me too. He certainly knew how bad his car was. It seemed to be certain that I should get a March next year without having to pay for it – anyway I had no more money, only unbelievable debts. At the nine hour race in South Africa in the autumn Robin Herd told me his plans for next year, what colour my car would be, what the gear box would be like and heaven knows what else. In December I went to Bicester to March, where Max Mosley declared : We've got no money for you to drive in Formula I, but you can drive in Formula II and take over the work of testing in Formula I. I was done for; March wanted Chris Amon, and I should test for him, that was the meaning of this 'offer', that I was good at testing. So much the March people had now realized.

'I was never before and I have never been since in such despair as then, when I journeyed home from Bicester. Even the idea of driving my car into a wall didn't seem too absurd. I was at the end of the road, I had debts of two million schillings, (500,000 of the original sum I had paid back, with starting money and touring car prizes), so two million of debts and no car, no contract for next year. The whole business only had a chance if I got on in my career – I could never get hold of that sort of money in a 'normal' profession, to pay back what I owed. I reckoned how long it would take me if I got a clerk's job. Taking interest into account, and allowing for a minimum to live on, it would take between forty and seventy years, according to the degree of optimism. This reckoning convinced me that resignation was the worst solution, because it wasn't really a way out. The only chance was to stay in motor racing; only there could I find any ground for hope to pay back my debts in a reasonable time, as well as keeping my goal before my eyes: to become an established Formula I driver.

'After I had reckoned it all up and thought it over I was a bit more confident, and prepared my next move. One thing was certain: I must find a solution which cost nothing, for another loan was unthinkable.

I approached the BRM chief, Louis Stanley, who was only interested in me if I brought money with me. So I gave him the impression that I could get some more sponsor money from the *Raiffeisenkasse*. In any case I was to go testing at Paul Ricard, and I made a good enough impression to keep Stanley's interest in me alive. He then offered me a contract;

my 'sponsor' (who didn't exist) would have to give BRM a lot of money, and he would get prize and starting money from BRM in return. I signed, because I had no choice, and changed the clauses about paying the 'sponsor' money so that the first payments were to fall due after BRM had paid me my starting money. So I took the money I got from them and sent it straight off by post in the name of my 'sponsor'. Enough to live on and to pay interest on my loan I got by driving touring-car races. The whole calculation had one catch in it : the third 'sponsor' payment to BRM couldn't be found with the best will in the world, so that in June a huge gap awaited me. As I was playing for such high stakes, I could and would not allow myself to be stopped by that. Perhaps a miracle would happen.'

The most lucrative job in 1973 was the touring-car races, where the fight between BMW and Ford escalated so that the best available drivers were needed. At some of these races you got a dozen Grand Prix drivers at the start. Lauda drove for the Alpina team, whose leader Dr Fritz Indra remembers :

'Although he certainly needed the money badly, he was tremendously keen on the driving. For instance he came to the six-hour race at Nürburgring with the ambition to beat Hans Stuck. Stuck was considered the greatest daredevil on the Ring, and a perfect touring-car specialist, and Niki found it stimulating to be able to disenchant him. Since Stuck was also driving a BMW there was a more or less direct comparison between them.

'Lauda drove on Saturday morning in 8.17 minutes, that was an unbelievably fabulous time for a touring car (at that time with 2-valve cylinder head!) Stuck took three seconds longer, not to speak of the others.'

The journalist Dieter Stappert and the photographer Dieter Finck on that Saturday morning : 'We were standing at the Pflanzgarten. Lauda came flying along, none of the wheels seemed to be going in the right direction, the whole BMW looked shaken under the stress of the way it was being driven. With a drift angle beyond what one would think possible he disappeared from our field of vision. We both had the same reaction : pack up and go, it seemed senseless to wait for any other car, it would be so colourless by comparison.'

Interesting that Lauda was once a real expert on the Nürburgring, and seemed to enjoy his drives in the Eifel very much. What changed his attitude to this race-course, which already before his bad accident he described as being too dangerous?

LAUDA : 'Simply the fact that a young driver takes some time and must experience certain things before he wakes up, as I've already described in this book. And then there's naturally an enormous difference between a BMW Coupé and a formula car – with a touring car you have a chance when there's an accident, so long as you can avoid head-on collisions.'

Fritz Indra on the subject of Lauda's achievement in 1973 : 'He inspired the whole team. The way he handled the mechanics, the trouble he took in the preparation of the car, electrified all those taking part. In that year Jacky Ickx also drove for us. He turned up a quarter of an hour before training, got into the car and then said he wasn't comfortable – that the seat and the pedals must be re-built. Things which Niki had been looking into for days with greatest care. And in the driving he was unbelievably aggressive, particularly in cases where it needed great courage to go flat out. That he would ever bother much about the safety of the circuit was not evident in those days, he drove on unsafe circuits like Brünn and remained perfectly relaxed. What struck you was how "clever" his best performances were. He often kept himself back, in practice, and awaited the right moment, and then really went flat out. He always thought more deeply than the others, and he also gave himself endless trouble preparing the race. He was more serious than most of his opponents – he never joined the Stuck and Quester circus, but kept himself apart.'

Indra, the technician, on Lauda's technical ability : 'You should have no illusions about the technical knowledge of Grand Prix drivers. Hardly any of them has a profound idea of technical connections. Even Lauda's technical knowledge doesn't go far, but of all the top drivers he is probably the one who can express himself most precisely about technical matters. When he gives the reason for difficulties as being "left front" you can be one hundred per cent sure that that's where the trouble lies. Therefore with him you get to the root of the trouble much more quickly. Without exactly knowing, he's got more "technical feel" than perhaps any other driver.'

As touring-car driver Lauda earned a lot. He drove wherever he was well paid, even grilling races like a 24-hour race on the Nürburgring. He got 5,000 DM starting money, and another 5,000 DM for winning. And he won often, sometimes two races in a week-end. This was urgently necessary, to pay what he owed and to finance his life and journeys. There was hardly anything over for the ever more threatening third 'sponsor' payment to BRM. All the same he had a somewhat more successful season than he had with March.

Niki Lauda on his season with BRM, spring 1973 : 'I drove well in Argentine and Brazil, and in South Africa I was to get my own car for the first time; up to now I'd had whatever car was left over after training. We drove tests at Kyalami and then "my own" car arrived from England. When we did the tests I was quicker than Regazzoni, who was then number one at BRM. I was faster than him all day, and the BRM people began to look silly : what's up with the Benjamin? Thereupon Regazzoni said his car was going badly, he wanted to have mine. There was of course nothing I could do about it, in a moment I had lost my car. In official practice I drove Regazzoni's car, and it was bad to drive because it under-steered badly. I got them to make a few adjustments, and the car went well. Then again during the whole practice I was faster than my team-mates Regazzoni and Beltoise, until Fire-stone came forward with special tyres – naturally only for Regazzoni and Beltoise. Therefore both were in front of me on the grid, despite the fact that I'd been the fastest man in the team. Unlike them, however, I made a marvellous start and was driving in the first group, until after one third of the race my engine blew up. Before that there'd been the collision in which Regazzoni would have lost his life, except that Hailwood pulled him out of the burning car. In any case, the race in South Africa changed my position within the team; at first with no great consequences, but they began to value me more. Then I got a fifth place at Zolder and the first world championship point of my life; a fortnight later came one of the key races of my career: the 1973 Monaco Grand Prix.

'The car was pretty good and I felt pleased. During Satur-day practice I was faster than ever before: second-best time, behind Cevert, in front of Stewart and the other astronauts. Because of the unusual heat the whole day was slower than the day before, so that I didn't get second place on the grid, but sixth, next to Fittipaldi, very thrilling for me. I can remember three scenes from the race. First the start, which I didn't make a hash of, but all the same Regazzoni came up from behind and passed me. That annoyed me very much, because I really hadn't reckoned with such a thing. In the next scene I see Cevert, he bangs against the curb-stone and damages a wheel. Then there was a terrific braking mistake by Regazzoni, I think his brakes weren't working properly, and I find myself in third place – behind Stewart and Fitti-paldi and directly in front of Jacky Ickx.

'For the first time I drove for a long time in the middle of the world class drivers. I can remember the feeling I had exactly, no excitement, only concentration; I kept saying to myself Look out, Look out, whatever happened I didn't want to make a mistake. I didn't feel like a fighter but like someone who, for heaven's sake, mustn't bungle. It was amazing that Ickx behind me was never a threat.

'After one third of the race the dream suddenly came to an end – differential damage which was surprising for BRM. I was madly disappointed, but I realized I'd given a show, that for the first time I'd driven in great style. This race had a direct consequence for me, and at the same time it was a delayed-action bomb. Stanley immediately took me as a non-paying driver in his team, and Enzo Ferrari had from then on a secret plan, to sign me up for next year – only two months went by before we first met.

'As to Stanley, I was saved at the right moment – I never knew how I could have managed the third 'sponsor' payment. The new contract with BRM had a clause that I should get starting money and prize money, and against that I must give him an option on the following year. (It was luck for me that the Marlboro lawyers were able to question this option). Stanley was a rather odd old fellow.

'The most memorable of all the little stories and funny things that I experienced with him happened about the middle of season in the Dorchester Hotel in London. Stanley had invited me to tea, everything was terribly grand. At this time I was already the unofficial number one in the team, but Stanley put upon me more than he did Regazzoni or Beltoise. I seized the opportunity and told him an important truth, namely that the BRM engines were hopeless – 'we need another 50 horse power, Mr Stanley!' This was certainly right, because it was awful the way all the others got the better of us. Stanley got up and excused himself and went out for about ten minutes. When he came back he said he'd had a call from 'Test House' and they'd told him they'd found another 25 h.p. – in the exhaust system. But when I sat in the car I realised at once that nothing had changed in the slightest. Looking back I feel that perhaps Stanley just went out to pee and that it was in the lavatory the idea of telephoning his people about an extra 25 h.p. 'in the exhaust system' occurred to him.

'The situation at BRM became ever more hopeless – we had no successes. I was naturally happy over my future with Ferrari and wanted to perform well for BRM meanwhile. At Monza I crashed into the barrier; apparently a broken wheel. Then followed a – for me – grotesque race, the Canadian Grand Prix at Mosport. The BRMs were no better and no worse than usual. Regazzoni had already been put on ice by Stanley; instead of him, Gethin drove. I was the fastest BRM driver in practice, in eighth place, Beltoise was sixteenth. The race started in the rain; and from the beginning I got further and further to the front. What is the matter, I thought, why are they all driving so slowly? I passed them like the very devil, and was suddenly out in the lead. Niki Lauda for the first time leading the Grand Prix field.

'Naturally it was plain to me that neither I nor BRM had worked this miracle, but that it was simply the Firestone tyres, which were so much better in the rain than the Goodyears of my opponents. It was grotesque, the way my lead got ever bigger – behind nobody emerged, nobody attacked, instead I got further and further in front. Then it cleared up and the track dried and I had to get a tyre change. Everything went with the usual speed – only I had the wrong tyres. In those days there were still 'intermediates', and our team manager Parnell had got those for me, although the surface was by now dry enough for ordinary slicks. The tyres were finished after a couple of laps, I had to go back into the pits to put the proper ones on, and in the last quarter of the race came the inevitable problem. This time it was the petrol pump.

'Telling Louis Stanley that I couldn't drive for him next season was my hardest job that autumn. It was very painful.'

One question remains : Niki, how does the financing of your career with borrowed money look in retrospect ?

LAUDA : 'Madness. The situation demanded that I risk everything. I had good luck, but I wouldn't do it again. If I had to take the same decision now, I should probably never be a racing driver. The chance of getting to the top in motor racing is so unbelievably small, that it's madness to try and do it with borrowed money. The stake and the odds against success are just too big.'

But that doesn't mean that you regret having forced your career through in this violent way ?

'No, for heaven's sake, I was lucky. But there was so much luck necessary that the way I did it is not to be repeated. It was an incredible, unique case, and I don't think it would be possible to do it in such a way again.'

Appendix

187 races in 10 years: All Niki Lauda's starts

1968

Moutain race Bad Mühllacken, Austria, 15.4
Cooper 1300, second place
Class winner Herbert Grünsteidl, Austria, Cooper
Overall winner Richard Gerin, Austria, Porsche 906

Mountain race Dobratsch, Austria, 28.4
Cooper 1300, class win
Overall winner Rudi Lins, Austria, Porsche 906

Mountain race Alpl, Austria, 5.5
Cooper 1300, class win
Overall winner Richard Gerin, Austria, Porsche 906

Mountain race Engelhartszell, Austria, 26.5
Cooper 1300, class win
Overall winner Gerhard Krammer, Austria, Brabham-Alfa

Mountain race Kasten-Viechtenstein, Austria, 9.6
Porsche 911, retired (accident)
Overall winner Dieter Schmied, Germany, Lotus 23

Airfield race Tulln-Langenlebarn, Austria, 14.7
Porsche 911, retired (engine)
Overall winner Klaus Reisch, Austria, Alfa-Romeo GTA

Koralpe-mountain race, Austria, 23.6
Porsche 911, class win
Overall winner Richard Gerin, Austria, Porsche 906

Mountain race Tauplitzalm, Austria, 4.8
Porsche 911, class win
Overall winner Giulio de Guidi, Switzerland, Cooper-ATS

Mountain race Stainz, Austria, 11.8
Porsche 911, class win
Overall winner Jochen Rindt, Austria, Brabham Formula 2

Mountain race Walding, Austria, 15.8
Porsche 911, class win
Overall winner Peter Peter, Austria, Porsche 906

Airfield race Zeltweg, 25.8
Porsche 911, overall winner

Airfield race Aspern, Austria, 6.10
Porsche 911, third place
Winner Ernst Furtmayer, Germany, BMW 2002

Kaimann Formula V : eighth place
Winner Erich Breinsberg, Austria, Kaimann

Mountain race Dopplerhütte, Austria, 27.10
Porsche 911 : eighth place
Kaimann : ninth place
Overall winner : Rudi Lins, Austria, Porsche 910

1969

Hockenheim, Germany, 12.4
Kaimann Formula V, fourth place
Winner Gerold Pankl, Austria, Austro Vau

Airfield race Aspern, Austria, 13.4
Kaimann Formula V, retired
Winner Peter Peter, Austria, Austro Vau

Belgrade, Yugoslavia, 20.4
Kaimann Formula V, second place
Winner Gerold Pankl, Austria, Austro Vau

Budapest, Hungary, 11.5
Kaimann Formula V, fourth place
Winner Alfred Vogelberger, Germany, Olympic

Hockenheim, Germany, 25.5
Kaimann Formula V, second place
Winner Erich Breinsberg, Austria, Kaimann

Mantorp Park, Sweden, 29.6
Kaimann Formula V, retired (petrol pump)
Winner Bertil Roos, Sweden, RPB

Sopron, Hungary, 6.7
Kaimann Formula V, winner

Airfield race Tulln-Langenlebarn, Austria, 13.7
Opel 1900, retired (engine)
Winner Peter Huber, Austria, Ford Escort TC

aimann Formula V, third place
inner Peter Peter, Austria, Austro Vau

sterreichring, Austria, 27.7
aimann Formula V, eighth place
inner Helmut Marko, Austria, McNamara

urburgring, Germany, 3.8
aimann Formula V, second place
inner Helmut Marko, Austria, McNamara

sterreichring, Austria, 10.8
uda/Stuppacher, Austria, Porsche 910, twenty-first place
inner Siffert/Ahrens, Switzerland/Germany, Porsche 917

izburgring, Austria, 21.9
imann Formula V, third place
nner Dieter Quester, Austria, Kaimann

-field race Innsbruck, Austria, 5.10
imann Formula V, second place
nner Erich Breinsberg, Austria, Kaimann

izburgring (Donaupokal), Austria, 12.10
imann Formula V, (retired)
nner Gerold Pankl, Austria, Austro Vau

-field race München-Neubiberg, Germany, 26.10
el 1900 : (retired)
imann Formula Vau : winner

•70

garo, France, 29.3
rmula 3 McNamara, retired (accident)
nner Jean-Pierre Jaussaud, France, Tecno

agny Cours, France, 3.5
rmula 3 McNamara, fifth place
nner Jean-Pierre Jaussaud, France, Tecno

ckenheim, Germany, 10.5
rmula 3 McNamara, retired (accident)
nner Hermann Unold, Germany, Tecno

sterreichring, Austria, 17.5
rmula 3 McNamara, sixth place
nner Freddy Kottulinsky, Lotus

inn, Czechoslovakia, 24.5
rmula 3 McNamara, second place
nner Jürg Dubler, Switzerland, Chevron

risring, Germany, 28.6
sche 908, eighth place
nner Jürgen Neuhaus, Germany, Porsche 917

ckenheim, Germany, 5.7
sche 908, twelfth place
nner Vic Elford, McLaren-Chevy

Formula 3 McNamara, fifth place
Winner Gianni Salvati, Italy, Tecno

Brands Hatch, GB, 17.7
Formula 3 McNamara, retired (accident)
Winner Mike Beuttler, GB, Brabham

Airfield race Diepholz, Germany, 19.7
Porsche 908; winner

Karlskoga, Sweden, 9.8
Formula 3 McNamara, fifth place
Winner Peter Hanson, GB, Chevron

Knutstorp, Sweden, 16.8
Formula 3 McNamara, retired, (accident)
Winner Ulf Svensson, Sweden, Brabham

Keimola, Finland, 23.8
Porsche 908, retired
Winner Gijs van Lennep, Holland, Porsche 917

Zandvoort, Holland, 30.8
Formula 3 McNamara, fourth place
Winner Jürg Dubler, Switzerland, Chevron

Zolder, Belgium, 6.9
Formula 3 McNamara, retired, (accident)
Winner James Hunt, GB, Lotus

Imola, Italy, 13.9
Lauda/Kottulinsky, Austria/Sweden, Porsche 908, fifth place
Winner Brian Redman, GB, Porsche 917

Thruxton, GB, 20.9
Porsche 908, fifth place
Winner Jürgen Neuhaus, Porsche 917

1,000 KM Oesterreichring, Marken-WM, Austria, 11.10
Lauda/Peter, Austria, Porsche 908, sixth place
Winners Siffert/Redman, Switzerland/GB, Porsche 917

Nürburgring, Germany, 18.10
Porsche 908, third place
Winner Helmut Kelleners, Germany, March-Chevy

Oesterreichring (Martha Grand National), Austria, 25.10
Porsche 908, winner

1971

Mallory Park, GB, 14.3
Formula 2 March/Ford, retired (petrol pump)
Winner Henri Pescarolo, France, March-Ford

Hockenheim, F-2-EM, Germany, 4.4
Formula 2 March/Ford, retired
Winner François Cevert, France, Tecno-Ford

Thruxton, F-2-EM, GB, 12.4
Formula 2 March-Ford tenth place
Winner Graham Hill, GB, Brabham-Ford

Nürburgring, F-2-EM, Germany, 2.5
Formula 2 March-Ford, sixth place
Winner François Cevert, France, Tecno-Ford

Jarama, F-2-EM, Spain, 16.5
Formula 2 March-Ford, seventh place
Winner Emerson Fittipaldi, Brazil, Lotus-Ford

Salzburgring, 2-EM, Austria, 23.5
Chevron-Ford (2-1 Sports car) winner

Crystal Palace, F-2-EM, GB, 31.5
Formula 2 March-Ford, failed to qualify
Winner Emerson Fittipaldi, Brazil, Lotus-Ford

Monza, Italy, 20.6
Formula 2 March-Ford, retired (gearbox)
Winner Dieter Quester, Austria, March-BMW

Rouen, F-2-EM, France, 27.6
Formula 2 March-Ford, fourth place
Winner Ronnie Peterson, Sweden, March-Ford

Nürburgring, TW-EM, Germany, 11.7
Lauda/Huber, Austria, Alpina-BMW Coupé, third place
Winners Marko/Glemser, Austria/Germany, Ford Capri RS

Spa-Francorchamps, TW-EM, Belgium, 24/25.7
Lauda/Larrousse, Austria/France, Alpina-BMW Coupé,
    retired (gearbox)
Winners Glemser/Soler-Roig, Germany/Ford Capri RS

Mantorp Park, F-2-EM, Sweden 8.8
Formula 2 March-Ford, thirteenth place
Winner Ronnie Peterson, Sweden, March-Ford

Austrian Grand Prix, Oesterreichring, 15.8
Formula 1 March, retired, (engine)
Winner Jo Siffert, Switzerland, BRM

Kinnekulle, Sweden, 22.8
Formula 2 March-Ford, sixth place
Winner Ronnie Peterson, Sweden, March-Ford

Brands Hatch, GB, 30.8
Formula 2 March-Ford, seventh place
Winner Ronnie Peterson, Sweden, March-Ford

Tulln-Langenlebarn, F-2-EM, Austria, 1.9
Formula 2 March-Ford, retired, (spun, unable to restart
    engine)
Winner Ronnie Peterson, Sweden, March-Ford

Albi, F-2-EM, France, 26.9
Formula 2 March-Ford, retired (front suspension)
Winner Emerson Fittipaldi, Brazil, Lotus-Ford

Vallelunga, F-2-EM, Italy, 10.10
Formula 2 March-Ford, seventh place
Winner Ronnie Peterson, Sweden, March-Ford

1972

Argentine Grand Prix, Buenos Aires, 23.1
Formula 1 March, eleventh place
Winner Jackie Stewart, GB, Tyrrell-Ford

South African Grand Prix, Kyalami, 4.3
Formula 1 March, seventh place
Winner Denny Hulme, New Zealand, McLaren-For

Mallory Park, F-2-EM, GB, 12.3
Formula 2 March-Ford, second place
Winner Dave Morgan, GB, Brabham-Ford

Oulton Park, GB, 31.3
Formula 2 March-Ford, winner

Thruxton, F-2-EM, GB, 3.4
Formula 2 March-Ford, third place
Winner Ronnie Peterson, Sweden, March-Ford

Hockenheim, F-2-EM, Germany, 16.4
Formula 2 March-Ford, retired, (engine)
Winner Jean-Pierre Jaussaud, France, Brabham-Fe

Spanish Grand Prix, Jarama, 1.5
Formula 1 March, retired (jammed accelerator)
Winner Emerson Fittipaldi, Brazil, Lotus-Ford

Monaco Grand Prix, Monte Carlo, 14.5
Formula 1 March, sixteenth place
Winner Jean Pierre Beltoise, France, BRM

Pau, F-2-EM, France, 7.5
Formula 2 March/Ford, retired (drive shaft)
Winner Peter Gethin, GB, Chevron-Ford

Brünn, TW-EM, Czechoslovakia, 21.5
Alpina-BMW, retired (engine)
Winner Dieter Glemser, Germany, Ford Capri

Crystal Palace, F-2-EM, GB, 29.5
Formula 2 March/Ford, retired (engine)
Winner Jody Scheckter, South Africa, McLaren-Fe

Belgian Grand Prix, Nivelles, 4.6
Formula 1 March, twelfth place
Winner Emerson Fittipaldi, Brazil, Lotus-Ford

Hockenheim, F-2-EM, Germany, 11.6
Formula 2 March-Ford, retired (engine)
Winner Emerson Fittipaldi, Lotus-Ford

Rouen, F-2-EM, France, 25.6
Formula 2 March-Ford, retired, (engine)
Winner Emerson Fittipaldi, Brazil, Lotus-Ford

Rome Prize, Vallelunga, Italy, 18.6
Formula 1 March, accident in training, unable to start
Winner Emerson Fittipaldi, Brazil, Lotus-Ford

French Grand Prix, Clermont-Ferrand, 2.7
Formula 1 March, retired (rear suspension)
Winner Jackie Stewart, GB, Tyrrell-Ford

Oesterreichring, F-2-EM, Austria, 9.7
Formula 2 March-Ford, retired (engine)
Winner Emerson Fittipaldi, Brazil, Lotus-Ford

English Grand Prix, Brands Hatch, 15.7
Formula 1 March, ninth place
Winner Emerson Fittipaldi, Brazil, Lotus-Ford

Imola, F-2-EM, Italy, 23.7
Formula 2 March-Ford, third place
Winner John Surtees, GB, Surtees-Ford

German Grand Prix, Nürburgring, 30.7
Formula 1 March, retired (leak in oil-tank)
Winner Jacky Ickx, Belgium, Ferrari

Mantorp Park, F-2-EM, Sweden, 6.8
Formula 2 March-Ford, retired (engine)
Winner Mike Hailwood, GB, Surtees-Ford

Austrian Grand Prix, Oesterreichring, 13.8
Formula 1 March, tenth place
Winner Emerson Fittipaldi, Brazil, Lotus-Ford

Zandvoort, TW-EM, Holland, 27.8
Lauda/Hezemans, Austria/Holland, Alpina-BMW-Coupé,
   third place
Winners Mass/Soler-Roig, Germany/Ford Capri RS

Salzburgring, F-2-EM, Austria, 3.9
Formula 2 March-Ford, sixth place
Winner Mike Hailwood, GB, Surtees-Ford

Italian Grand Prix, Monza, 10.9
Formula 1 March, thirteenth place
Winner Emerson Fittipaldi, Brazil, Lotus-Ford

Oulton Park, GB, 16.9
Formula 2 March-Ford, second place
Winner Ronnie Peterson, Sweden, March-Ford

Canadian Grand Prix, Mosport, 24.9
Formula 1 March, retired (disqualified)
Winner Jackie Stewart, GB, Tyrrell-Ford

Hockenheim, F-2-EM, Germany, 1.10
Formula 2 March-Ford, ninth place
Winner Tim Schenken, Australia, Brabham-Ford

USA Grand Prix, Watkins Glen, 8.10
Formula 1 March seventeenth place
Winner Jackie Stewart, GB, Tyrrell-Ford

9-h-Kyalami, South Africa, 4.11
Lauda/Scheckter, Austria/South Africa, March BMW,
   fourth place
Winners Regazzoni/Merzario, Switzerland/Italy, Ferrari

1973

Argentine Grand Prix, Buenos Aires, 28.1
Formula 1 BRM, retired (engine)
Winner Emerson Fittipaldi, Brazil, Lotus-Ford

Brazilian Grand Prix, Interlagos, 11.2
Formula 1 BRM, eighth place
Winner Emerson Fittipaldi, Brazil, Lotus-Ford

South African Grand Prix, Kyalami, 3.3
Formula 1 BRM, retired (engine, broken con rod)
Winner Jackie Stewart, GB, Tyrrell-Ford

Race of Champions, Brands Hatch, GB, 18.3
Formula 1 BRM, retired (battery, tyres)
Winner Peter Gethin, GB, Chevron F 5000

4-h-Monza, TW-EM, Italy, 25.3
Lauda/Muir, Alpina-BMW-Coupé, winners

Airfield race Aspern, Austria, 1.4
BMW 2002 Gr. 1, retired (tyres)
Winner Dieter Quester, Austria, BMW 2002/Gr. 1

Daily Express Trophy, Silverstone, GB, 8.4
Formula 1 BRM, fifth place
Winner Jackie Stewart, GB, Tyrrell-Ford

Spanish Grand Prix, Barcelona, 29.4
Formula 1 BRM, retired (tyres)
Winner Emerson Fittipaldi, Brazil, Lotus-Ford

Coupe de Spa, Belgium, 5.5
Alpina BMW Coupé, winner

1000 km Spa, Marken-WM, Belgium, 6.5
Lauda/Stuck, Austria/Germany, Alpina BMW Coupé,
   seventh place
Winners Bell/Hailwood, GB, Gulf Mirage Ford

Monaco Grand Prix, Monte Carlo, 3.6
Formula 1 BRM, retired (gearbox/clutch)
Winner Jackie Stewart, GB, Tyrrell-Ford

Belgian Grand Prix, Zolder, 20.5
Formula 1 BRM, fifth place
Winner Jackie Stewart, GB, Tyrrell-Ford

Swedish Grand Prix, Anderstorp, 17.6
Formula 1 BRM, thirteenth place
Winner Denny Hulme, New Zealand, McLaren-Ford

24-h-Nürburgring, Germany, 23/24.6
Lauda/Joisten, Austria/Germany, Alpina BMW Coupé
winners

French Grand Prix, Le Castellet, 1.7
Formula 1 BRM, ninth place
Winner Ronnie Peterson, Sweden, Lotus-Ford

6-h-Nürburgring, TW-EM, Germany, 8.7
Lauda/Joisten, Austria/Germany, Alpina BMW Coupé,
third place
Winners Stuck/Amon, Germany/New Zealand, BMW CSL

English Grand Prix, Silverstone, 14.7
Formula 1 BRM, twelfth place
Winner Peter Revson, US, McLaren-Ford

Airfield race Diepholz, Germany, 15.7
Alpina BMW Coupé, retired (engine)
Winner Rolf Stommelen, Germany, Ford Capri RS

Dutch Grand Prix, Zandvoort, 29.7
Formula 1 BRM, retired (tyres/petrol pressure)
Winner Jackie Stewart, GB, Tyrrell-Ford

German Grand Prix, Nürburgring, 5.8
Formula 1 BRM, retired, (accident)
Winner Jackie Stewart, GB, Tyrrell-Ford

Austrian Grand Prix, Oesterreichring, 19.8
Does not start, owing to injured hand from Nürburgring
accident
Winner Ronnie Peterson, Sweden, Lotus-Ford

Italian Grand Prix, Monza, 9.9
Formula 1 BRM, retired (accident)
Winner Ronnie Peterson, Sweden, Lotus-Ford

Canadian Grand Prix, Mosport, 23.9
Formula 1 BRM, retired (differential)
Winner Peter Revson, USA, McLaren-Ford

Airfield race Innsbruck, Austria, 30.9
Group 1 BMW 2002; class winner

USA Grand Prix, Watkins Glen, 7.10
Formula 1 BRM, eighteenth place
Winner Ronnie Peterson, Sweden, Lotus-Ford

End of Season, Oesterreichring, 14.10
Ford Capri RS, class winner

1974

Argentine Grand Prix, Buenos Aires, 13.1
Formula 1 Ferrari, second place
Winner Denny Hulme, New Zealand, McLaren Ford

Brazilian Grand Prix, Interlagos, 27.1
Formula 1 Ferrari, retired (engine)
Winner Emerson Fittipaldi, Brazil, McLaren-Ford

Race of Champions, Brands Hatch, GB, 17.3
Formula 1 Ferrari, second place
Winner Jacky Ickx, Belgium, Lotus-Ford

South African Grand Prix, Kyalami, 30.3
Formula 1 Ferrari, retired
Winner Carlos Reutemann, Argentine, Brabham-Fo

Touring car EM Salzburgring, Austria, 14.4
Lauda/Mass, Austria/Germany, Ford Capri RS, ret
(engine)
Winners Stuck/Ickx, Germany/Belgium, BMW, 3.0

Spanish Grand Prix, Jarama, 28.4
Formula 1 Ferrari, winner

Belgian Grand Prix, Nivelles, 12.5
Formula 1 Ferrari, second place
Winner Emerson Fittipaldi, Brazil, McLaren-Ford

1000-km Nürburgring (Marken-WM), Germany, 19
Lauda/Mass, Austria/Germany, Ford Capri RS, ret
(lost a wheel)
Winners Beltoise/Jarier, France, Matra

Monaco Grand Prix, Monte Carlo, 26.5
Formula 1 Ferrari, retired (ignition)
Winner Ronnie Peterson, Sweden, Lotus-Ford

Swedish Grand Prix, Anderstorp, 9.6
Formula 1 Ferrari, retired (rear suspension)
Winner Jody Scheckter, South Africa, Tyrrell-Ford

Dutch Grand Prix, Zandvoort, 23.6
Formula 1 Ferrari, winner

French Grand Prix, Dijon, 7.7
Formula 1 Ferrari, second place
Winner Ronnie Peterson, Sweden, Lotus-Ford

6-h Nürburgring (TW-EM) Germany, 14.7
Lauda/Glemser/Hezemans, Austria/Germany/Ho
Ford-Capri RS, second place
Winners Heyer/Ludwig, Germany, Zakspeed-Escor

English Grand Prix, Brands Hatch, 20.7
Formula 1 Ferrari, ninth place
Winner Jody Scheckter, South Africa, Tyrrell-Ford

German Grand Prix, Nürburgring, 4.8
Formula 1 Ferrari, retired (accident)
Winner Clay Regazzoni, Switzerland, Ferrari

Austrian Grand Prix, Oesterreichring, 18.8
Formula 1 Ferrari, retired (valve spring)
Winner Carlos Reutemann, Argentina, Brabham-Ford

Italian Grand Prix, Monza, 8.9
Formula 1 Ferrari, retired, (engine)
Winner Ronnie Peterson, Sweden, Lotus-Ford

Norisring, Germany, 15.9
Ford Capri, sixth place
Winner Hans-Joachim Stuck, Germany, BMW 3,0 CSL

Canadian Grand Prix, Mosport, 22.9
Formula 1 Ferrari, retired (accident)
Winner Emerson Fittipaldi, Brazil, McLaren-Ford

USA Grand Prix, Watkins Glen, 6.10
Formula I Ferrari, retired (shock absorber)
Winner Carlos Reutemann, Argentine, Brabham-Ford

1975

Argentine Grand Prix, Buenos Aires, 12.1
Formula 1 Ferrari, sixth place
Winner Emerson Fittipaldi, McLaren-Ford

Brazilian Grand Prix, Interlagos, 26.1
Formula 1 Ferrari, fifth place
Winner Carlos Pace, Brazil, Brabham-Ford

South African Grand Prix, Kyalami, 1.3
Formula 1 Ferrari, fifth place
Winner Jody Scheckter, South Africa, Tyrrell-Ford

Spanish Grand Prix, Barcelona, 27.4
Formula 1 Ferrari, retired (accident)
Winner Jochen Mass, Germany, McLaren-Ford

Monaco Grand Prix, Monte Carlo, 11.5
Formula 1 Ferrari, winner

Belgian Grand Prix, Zolder, 25.5
Formula 1 Ferrari, winner

Swedish Grand Prix, Anderstorp, 8.6
Formula 1 Ferrari, winner

Dutch Grand Prix, Zandvoort, 22.6
Formula 1 Ferrari, second place
Winner James Hunt, GB, Hesketh-Ford

French Grand Prix, Le Castellet, 7.7
Formula 1 Ferrari, winner

German Grand Prix, Nürburgring, 3.8
Formula 1 Ferrari, third place
Winner Carlos Reutemann, Argentine, Brabham-Ford

Austrian Grand Prix, Oesterreichring, 17.8
Formula 1 Ferrari, sixth place
Winner Vittorio Brambilla, Italy, March-Ford

English Grand Prix, Silverstone, 19.7
Formula 1 Ferrari, eighth place
Winner Emerson Fittipaldi, Brazil, McLaren Ford

Italian Grand Prix, Monza, 7.9
Formula 1 Ferrari, third place
Winner Clay Regazzoni, Switzerland, Ferrari

USA Grand Prix, Watkins Glen, 5.10
Formula 1 Ferrari, winner

1976

Brazilian Grand Prix, Interlagos, 25.1
Formula 1 Ferrari, winner

South African Grand Prix, Kyalami, 6.3
Formula 1 Ferrari, winner

USA/West Grand Prix, Long Beach, 28.3
Formula 1 Ferrari, second place
Winner Clay Regazzoni, Switzerland, Ferrari

Spanish Grand Prix, Jarama, 2.5
Formula 1 Ferrari, winner

Belgian Grand Prix, Zolder, 15.5
Formula 1 Ferrari, winner

Monaco Grand Prix, Monte Carlo, 30.5
Formula 1 Ferrari, winner

Swedish Grand Prix, Anderstorp, 13.6
Formula 1 Ferrari, third place
Winner Jody Scheckter, South Africa, Tyrrell-Ford

French Grand Prix, Le Castellet, 4.7
Formula 1 Ferrari, retired, (engine)
Winner James Hunt, GB, McLaren-Ford

English Grand Prix, Brands Hatch, 18.7
Formula 1 Ferrari, second place
Winner James Hunt, GB, McLaren-Ford

German Grand Prix, Nürburgring, 1.8
Formula 1 Ferrari, retired, (accident)
Winner James Hunt, GB, McLaren-Ford

Austrian Grand Prix, Oesterreichring, 15.8
Does not start
Winner John Watson, Ireland, Penske-Ford

Dutch Grand Prix, Zandvoort, 29.8
Does not start
Winner James Hunt, GB, McLaren-Ford

Italian Grand Prix, Monza, 12.9
Formula 1 Ferrari, fourth place
Winner Ronnie Peterson, Sweden, March-Ford

Canadian Grand Prix, Mosport, 3.10
Formula 1 Ferrari, eighth place
Winner James Hunt, GB, McLaren Ford

USA/East Grand Prix, Watkins Glen, 10.10
Formula 1 Ferrari, third place
Winner James Hunt, GB, McLaren-Ford

Japanese Grand Prix, Fuji, 24.10
Formula 1 Ferrari, gave up
Winner Mario Andretti, USA, Lotus-Ford

1977
Argentine Grand Prix, Buenos Aires, 9.1
Formula 1 Ferrari, retired, (fuel injection)
Winner Jody Scheckter, South Africa, Wolf-Ford

Brazilian Grand Prix, Interlagos, 23.1
Formula 1 Ferrari, third place
Winner Carlos Reutemann, Argentine, Ferrari

South African Grand Prix, Kyalami, 5.3
Formula 1 Ferrari, winner

USA/West Grand Prix, Long Beach, 3.4
Formula 1 Ferrari, second place
Winner Mario Andretti, USA, Lotus-Ford

Spanish Grand Prix, Jarama, 8.5
Formula 1 Ferrari, does not start, (injury to ribs)
Winner Mario Andretti, USA, Lotus-Ford

Monaco Grand Prix, Monte Carlo, 22.5
Formula 1 Ferrari, second place
Winner Jody Scheckter, South Africa, Wolf-Ford

Belgian Grand Prix, Zolder, 5.6
Formula 1 Ferrari, second place
Winner Gunnar Nilsson, Sweden, Lotus-Ford

Swedish Grand Prix, Anderstorp, 19.6
Formula 1 Ferrari, gave up
Winner Jacques Laffite, France, Ligier-Matra

French Grand Prix, Dijon, 3.7
Formula 1 Ferrari, fifth place
Winner Mario Andretti, USA, Lotus-Ford

English Grand Prix, Silverstone, 16.7
Formula 1 Ferrari, second place
Winner James Hunt, GB, McLaren-Ford

German Grand Prix, Hockenheimring, 31.7
Formula 1 Ferrari, winner

Austrian Grand Prix, Oesterreichring, 14.8
Formula 1 Ferrari, second place
Winner Alan Jones, Australia, Shadow-Ford

Dutch Grand Prix, Zandvoort, 28.7
Formula 1 Ferrari, winner

Italian Grand Prix, Monza, 11.9
Formula I Ferrari, second place
Winner Mario Andretti, USA, Lotus-Ford

USA/East Grand Prix, Watkins Glen, 2.10
Formula 1 Ferrari, fourth place
Winner James Hunt, GB, MacLaren-Ford

Canadian Grand Prix, Mosport, 9.10
Does not start
Winner Jody Scheckter, South Africa, Wolf-Ford

Japanese Grand Prix, Fuji, 23.10
Does not start
Winner James Hunt, GB, McLaren-Ford

Niki Lauda

THE ART AND SCIENCE OF GRAND PRIX DRIVING

Contents